MAAATE!
Bribe-Proofing
the
Public Purse
Against
Good Blokes

Bernie Dowling

MAAATE! Bribe-Proofing the Public Purse Against Good Blokes

Copyright © 2017 Bernie Dowling and Bent Banana Books

All rights reserved. No part of this book may be reproduced, stored in a retrieval system, or transmitted, in any form or by any means without the prior written permission of the publisher, nor be otherwise circulated in any form of binding or cover other than that in which it is published and without a similar condition being imposed on the subsequent purchaser.

First published in 2017 by Bent Banana Books

Post to 24 Lorraine Court Lawnton Queensland 4501 Australia

Email bentbananabooks@gmail.com Phone 61 7 3889 2118

A CiP catalogue record for this book is available from the Australian National Library. *ISBN* **978-0-9953947-5-9 (paperback)**

Cover design: Ian Curr

Front Cover Art *Avarice* by Jesus Solana

MAAATE!
Bribe-Proofing
the
Public Purse
Against
Good Blokes

Bernie Dowling

Tall tales and true from the annals of a journo reporting on City Hall
And
From the Operation Belcarra corruption inquiry into Moreton Bay, Ipswich, Gold Coast, and Logan City councils

*The rain it raineth on the just
And also on the unjust fella;
But chiefly on the just, because
The unjust hath the just's umbrella.*

– Charles Bowen, 19th century Lord Justice of Appeal.

Preface

Professor Graeme Orr

'IN THE RACE OF LIFE, always back self-interest. At least you know it's trying'. That saying of Jack Lang, a renegade Labor Premier of NSW, was also a favourite of former Labor Prime Minister Paul Keating.

Most people who enter politics do so for noble reasons. They start wanting to achieve things in the public interest, motivated by their political philosophy. Yes, they are egoistical, but you have to be to put yourself in the public eye.

But over time, systemic risks come into play. From those risks are shaped the familiar figure of the self-serving minister or party apparatchik. The type who takes campaign donations which have only one purpose – to buy someone privileged access to power. In the worst case, the occasional political figure is personally corrupted.

None of this happens in a vacuum. It happens when those with wealth seek to use it in ways that unduly influence or distort representation in the public interest.

Politics is not meant to be a business. But, inescapably, it is a competitive game. And it is a game that requires resources. There may be shire councils in outback Queensland where an independent with a photocopier can canvass the electorate on the cheap.

In south-east Queensland, however, local government is becoming big business. Both in terms of the cost of campaigns and – of course – in the money hinging on decisions. Especially decisions about land planning and development in a booming corner of the world.

We have long had criminal laws against bribery. And increasingly, the law is regulating political finance. Queensland is embarking on a national first, a system of online, real-time disclosure of donations to candidates, councillors, and mayors. In chapter 21, this book offers suggestions to tighten those laws.

But in this realm, the law can only do so much. Systemic risks must be met by systemic solutions. The work of a robust anti-corruption commission – as reported in this book – is one such response.

The media, too, has a big role to play. I have spent years helping explain the law to journalists and the public. Too often we think of the media as national TV and the big mastheads of Fairfax and Murdoch.

But it is local journalism, especially newspapers and radio, that has consistently and most impressed me. Close to the events they report on, a good local reporter is amongst the best of investigatory journalists.

Bernie Dowling has been one such a person. He has worked as a journalist for over twenty years in the Ipswich then Moreton Bay Region, covering every election – for council, state and national representatives in those areas – in those twenty years.

In this book he chronicles and comments on evidence about political practices and cultures that deserve critical attention. And which deserve legal and cultural responses.

Ultimately facts do not speak for themselves. They are important. We surely need facts to overcome the tide of spin and fake news that clogs the 24/7 news cycle, especially on social media.

Local government is often touted as the form of democracy 'closest to the people'. It can still be, though it is challenging when – for efficiency and regional planning – councils have amalgamated and grown in size.

But facts only speak when we listen. The other half of healthy politics is an engaged citizenry.

If you are reading even this far into this book, you are a member of the Republic of People willing to take the time to focus on politics and current affairs.

Read, learn, weigh your own opinions. And encourage others to do the same.

**– Graeme Orr, Professor of Law,
University of Queensland**

Introduction

IN 2017 A MAN NAMED PAUL PISASALE is facing criminal charges including corruption in public office, extortion, assault, perjury, and attempting to pervert justice. In 2016, Paul Pisasale, pronounced Pis-ar-lee, was re-elected Mayor of the Queensland City of Ipswich with 83.45 per cent of the popular vote. In 2012 Mr Pisasale was re-elected Mayor with 87.81 per cent of the vote.

Mr Pisasale resigned due to ill-health in 2017 just before the first batch of charges were laid against him. He later threatened to contest the by-election his resignation created. Right up to the week before nominations closed he repeated his threat but was finally dissuaded from nominating by family members. A voter poll was taken after Mr Pisasale decided not to run but before the by-election. Had he contested the ballot, Mr Pisasale would have won comfortably. While the vote likely would have been different after a vigorous election campaign, it does show how difficult it is to dislodge an incumbent mayor.

In late 2015, a colleague and I, working for the *Pine Rivers Press*, began a close investigation of Moreton Futures Trust, a third-party supporter of Allan Sutherland when he was re-elected Mayor at the 2012 Moreton Bay Regional Council election. We were not encouraged by our editors as they considered our investigations could interfere with our other journalism on our community newspaper. The stories we wrote were all rejected as not passing the tests for possible defamation.

Something is broken at councils in south-east Queensland. By 2017, it could not be ignored. The Crime and Corruption Commission (CCC), an independent investigator created by State Parliament, called an inquiry to investigate the conduct of the 2016 elections for the councils of Moreton Bay Region, Ipswich, and the Gold Coast. Moreton Bay was a late addition to the inquiries dubbed Operation Belcarra after the Electoral Commission of Queensland referred certain matters including those involving Moreton Futures Trust to the CCC. Logan City Council was added to the brief after the hearings began.

Two witnesses at Operation Belcarra – Dr John Ryan and Kirby Leeke – mentioned our attempts in late 2015 and early 2016 to uncover information on Moreton Futures Trust.

I had been pestering the Electoral Commission about the trust including the fact that the name of trustee Dr Ryan should have been on the disclosure form and was not. I also inquired why Dr Ryan's transfer of more than $20,000 from the Friends of Pine Rivers third party to Moreton Futures Trust was not disclosed. A third party receives donations which it passes on to political candidates. Why do we need third parties? That's a good question. Another question I had of the Electoral Commission of Queensland was whether one organisation in Moreton Bay Region had acted as an undisclosed third party at the 2012 election. Since the emergence of the Local Government Electoral Act 2011, no one has been prosecuted for breaches of it.

Operation Belcarra is looking at the issues of third party donors, candidates working together in an undeclared group to help their electoral prospects, breaches of campaign financial recordings, and voting in council on matters involving donors.

In this book, I present the evidence of witnesses and suggest ways to mend broken councils. I have abridged the evidence to exclude repetition and to present what I consider the most pertinent and fascinating information and opinions. I have not changed the construction of questions or answers. Full transcripts are available by Googling 'Operation Belcarra'.

I have enlivened these accounts with insider tales of my robust exchanges with councillors and developers and other characters in our political comedy drama.

There is an old saying: You can't fight city hall. I do not subscribe to that. Now is the time for good citizens to fight city hall to ensure it is filled with incorruptible community representatives.

– Bernie Dowling, 2017

1

GOD MADE ADAM who went to the Archangel Mick to ask for a mate. 'Be an angel, Mick,' Adam said. 'Ask God if I can have a mate.'

The Archangel Mick didn't even have to think about it. 'What's in it for me?' he asked.

I have been covering elections – Federal, State and Local Government – in Australia for more than twenty years. But it was at the 2008 Moreton Bay Regional Council election that I had my first run-in with the good-bloke network, the mate mob.

Some candidates were funded by a third-party organisation called Advancing Moreton Leadership. For some reason or other, in Queensland Australia, we didn't have real-time reporting of political donations, so months after the election, I set about tracking down this Advancing Moreton Leadership mob.

They were a humble lot and did not want acknowledgement for their selfless act of helping to keep the good ship *Democracy* afloat. The way the system worked was that likeminded fans of democracy, good government, and Advancing Moreton Leadership, gave to what was known as a third party which in turn shrewdly judged who were the best election candidates to receive the donations.

What can I say: complicating political things seemed a good idea at the time.

As it turned out, property development was the industry, resplendent with good corporate citizens, most eager to donate to Advancing Moreton Leadership and other third parties helping to bail out a leaky *Democracy*. As they always do, the haters among the citizens following politics resented the good deeds of developers. The trouble makers called for their sissy favourite, public accountability. Humility was the biggest impediment to public accountability as the donors gave under (often) obscure business names to the third party, which in turn hid in the bushes of organisational registration.

As determined as they were to remain anonymous, we journalists were zealous in our efforts to give all involved their rightful places in the sun. I found Advancing Moreton Leadership was tied to a conservative political party committed to keeping fiendish socialists and environmentalists out of local government.

One of the Advancing Moreton Leadership donors was Bazza, a businessman given a long-term favourable lease agreement on Council land because his business was deemed tourism friendly.

Bazza gave money to the third party which in turn gave money to candidate Charlie Brown. Bazza donated directly to candidate Joseph Cable. The recipients Brown and Cable were both on the Council working group which had brokered the favourable lease to Bazza.

I asked Bazza why he donated to Cable. 'Joe's a good bloke,' he said. 'He got me into riding a bike to lose weight.'

Bazza volunteered some more information on his services to democracy.

'The way you are sniffin' around, I better tell you I handed out how-to-vote cards for Clifford Bradshaw (a major beneficiary of Advancing Moreton Leadership.)

'Cliff's a good bloke,' Bazza said.

How did he meet Bradshaw?

'I met Cliffie through Charlie Brown and found him to be a good bloke.'

2

I'D LIKE TO THINK my colleague, Walter Burns, and I had a hand in inciting part of the 2017 Crime and Corruption Commission (CCC) hearing into four 2016 south-east Queensland council elections, one being that of Moreton Bay Region.

It was Walter who, in 2015, developed a keen interest in Moreton Futures Trust, a third-party active at the 2012 Moreton Bay Regional Council elections. Walter knew I was interested in earlier third parties, Advancing Moreton Leadership, active in 2008, and Friends of Pine Rivers, which was active at the 2004 election for Pine Rivers Shire.

In 2008, Pine Rivers Shire, Caboolture Shire, and Redcliffe City amalgamated to form Moreton Bay Region. It was a dumb idea and that was pretty obvious when you considered the new Council was bigger than Sydney's or Melbourne's. Sydney and Melbourne are the two Big Smokes of Australia but those cities are subdivided into many councils. My suspicion was the Queensland State Government amalgamated the councils to create one possibly truculent local government instead of three. Also, big councils might relieve the state of some portions of substantial financial burdens. This proved true of Moreton Bay Regional Council which contributed $100 million towards the Redcliffe Peninsula railway line and more than $50 million towards establishing the Petrie university campus. Historically public contribution towards rail and university infrastructure has been within the domain of state governments, sometimes assisted by the Feds.

After amalgamation, the number of councillors was reduced but those who remained had their salaries substantially increased. The increased pay reflected the difficulty of councillors personally servicing enlarged divisions, called wards in other council areas. Some other councils were undivided, meaning councillors shared overall responsibility rather than for certain geographical areas. The councils investigated by Operation Belcarra – Moreton Bay, Gold Coast, Ipswich, and Logan City – had divisions.

The burden of large divisions was mitigated by the neat trick mobile phones did. On any given Councillor's screen, the name of a caller would pop up and the Councillor could choose whether to answer or deploy to a message bank which said the humble civil servant was busy servicing the community and would ring back. A couple of Councillors chose to ignore calls in my presence which annoyed me. I would have preferred to pause the interviews while the Councillors attended to the concerns of their callers. I myself was finding it increasingly difficult to get a live Councillor on the al-capone. Maybe it was just me, a pesky journo.

Adding to my woes of unrequited communication was the habit of my leaving a message on a councillor's phone, only to have my query answered, after a fashion, by a member of the Council media spin team. So much for 'your independent councillor' which they love to blare from their how-to-vote card, come election time.

To introduce a technical point, Moreton Bay Council savagely warns their public servants against speaking to journalists. The Council's philosophical argument is public servants are unelected and hence should not speak on behalf of the Council. Except it seems in the case of those Councillors who have the media team speak on their behalf. From my experience the mayor or an agent of the mayor vets most media releases, restricting independence of councillors.

In 2015/16, Walter and I talked with some of the future CCC witnesses and we were lucky enough to reach out to Professor Henry Higgins, a sharp legal mind on the subject of election laws. Professor Higgins told us some aspects of the interaction of Moreton Futures Trust and candidates for Council could be a bit dodgy legal-wise. I passed on our suspicions to the Electoral Commission of Queensland which in turn passed on its own concerns to the CCC.

3

I HAD A PARTICULARLY BAD DAY with the CMC, a decade ago.

Queensland has had a three-lettered thrice-iterated corruption-busting commission since 1989. It began as the Criminal Justice Commission (CJC) which sprang from the 1987–89 Fitzgerald Inquiry into police corruption.

It was renamed the Crime and Misconduct Commission (CMC) in 2002 and, in 2014, rebadged again to its present moniker of the Crime and Corruption Commission (CCC).

A decade ago, I sent a complaint to the middle one, the CMC, about what I considered illegality by a Councillor and a subsequent cover-up. Three days later I received a phone call from the Council CEO who said the CMC had closed its investigation.

I rang the CMC which confirmed the decision conveyed by the council officer. The CMC had referred my complaint about Council to Council which declared an emergency meeting of full Council. That meeting, closed to the public, found my complaint had no substance and the CEO informed the CMC of the decision. One councillor told me they were all intimidated by an outside party invited to the meeting into rendering a unanimous verdict which pardoned a crime. I never troubled the CMC with an official whinge after that.

Memories of my ill-fated complaint came back in October 2016 when the CCC held a two-day public hearing on whether we journos should be barred from publishing corruption complaints during the course of inquiries and only be allowed access to negative findings by the CMC.

It seemed that whingers had made excessive complaints about the council elections of March 2016. Complaints against candidates, mostly sitting councillors, were lodged concerning 29 of Queensland's 77 Councils. Most of the allegations were found to be wrong but that is not unusual as only two in a hundred CCC complaints proceed to formal investigations. Many, as in my case a decade earlier, are sent to the organisation complained about. Administrative convenience over-rides traditional advice not to let Caesar judge Caesar.

The CCC held the inquiry into restricting publication of complaints as it was concerned that the good names of councillors might be sullied by baseless whinges. Let's put this assault on character in perspective. In the 17 years I have covered council elections in the Pine Rivers area, only two sitting Councillors have lost their seats, both in the first amalgamated Council of 2008. Former Pine Rivers Councillors had to lose at the amalgamated Council elections of 2008 because four former office holders stood in two divisions. Two won and two lost. During that same period, 17 years from 2000, no sitting councillor in Ipswich ever lost their seat. On this evidence, the reputation of councillors is robust enough to withstand the rough and tumble of public criticism.

It is an offence to lodge a false or vexatious complaint with the CCC but the commission did not go so far as to say the complaints thrown out about the 2016 council elections were mostly of that nature.

I believe there are three main reasons why the volume of complaints about councils has risen. The baby boomer retirees have time on their hands despite their commitment to volunteering. Second, they have a keen sense of social justice. Third, in February 2017, Transparency International released its annual global corruption index which ranked Australia in 13th place for the second year running, down from eighth in 2012. (FYI, Denmark and New Zealand are tied for first as the least corrupt, and the United States is 18th.)

Four of the 29 Councils with complaints found themselves worthy of a full-blown public hearing beginning in April 2017. Pesky journos were allowed in. The four Councils were the Gold Coast, Logan City, Ipswich, and Moreton Bay Region. Moreton Bay, and Ipswich, this book is mostly about you.

Official release #1: April 2017
Operation Belcarra Inquiry
Terms of Reference
CONTEXT: Following the Queensland local government elections on 19 March 2016, the

Queensland Crime and Corruption Commission (CCC) received a number of allegations about the conduct of candidates for several councils. These allegations identified a number of possible breaches of the Local Government Electoral Act 2011 (LGE Act.) These allegations also identified practices that give rise to potential corruption risks, or may otherwise undermine transparency, integrity and public confidence not only in the 2016 elections, but in local government more generally.

The CCC established Operation Belcarra to investigate the allegations.

Objectives of the public hearing

Pursuant to sections 176 and 177 of the Crime and Corruption Act 2001, the Commission authorises and approves the holding of public hearings in relation to Operation Belcarra.

The CCC public hearing is:

1) investigating whether candidates in the Gold Coast, Moreton Bay and/or Ipswich 2016 local government elections. (Logan City was added after hearings began.)

a) advertised or fundraised for the election as an undeclared group of candidates, an offence contrary to section 183 of the LGE Act.

b) provided an electoral funding and financial disclosure return that was false or misleading in a material particular, an offence contrary to section 195 of the LGE Act.

c) have not operated a dedicated bank account during the candidates' disclosure period to receive and/or pay funds related to the candidates' election campaign, an offence contrary to section 126 of the LGE Act.

2) examining issues or practices that are relevant to the identification of actual or perceived corruption risks in relation to the conduct of candidates and third parties at local government elections, including issues or practices relating to groups of candidates, independence of candidates, election gifts and funding, conflicts of interest or material personal interests by councillors.

3) examining strategies or reforms to prevent or decrease actual or perceived corruption risks in relation to conduct of candidates and third parties at local government elections.

Public report

The CCC will issue a public report on the outcomes of Operation Belcarra.

(The report was handed down to State Parliament on October 4, 2017. I summarise most of the CCC recommendations later in this book. You can compare their recommendations to mine which I devised before the Operation Belcarra report was handed down. I generously allowed myself wider terms of reference than those of the CCC.)

The hearing commenced on Tuesday April 18, 2017, with CCC Chair Alan MacSporran QC as Presiding Officer. Council Assisting, who interviewed the witnesses, was Glen Rice QC. Both the PO and CA – be prepared to enter a world of acronyms – have backgrounds in criminal law.

QC stands for Queen's Council. Queen Elizabeth II of Great Britain appoints lawyers in her former colony of Australia as 'Her Majesty's Counsel learned in the law'. How Queen Elizabeth knows the competence and erudition of every lawyer in a foreign country is marvellous. For our purposes here, let's just acknowledge Mr MacSporran and Mr Rice are brainy legal blokes.

4

MORETON FUTURES TRUST was the hot topic at Day 3 of the Crime and Corruption Commission (CCC) hearing into the 2016 council elections of Moreton Bay, the Gold Coast, and Ipswich, with Logan City yet to be tacked on. The cast of the Operation Belcarra drama gathered at Green Square North in an environmentally awarded commercial tower in Fortitude Valley, an inner-city suburb of Brisbane.

It is only fitting the descendant of the 1987–89 Fitzgerald Inquiry is housed in a sanitised Fortitude Valley. Much of inquiry chief Tony Fitzgerald's field of vision on the eve of the naughty nineteen-nineties was of a more robust Fortitude Valley of old where illegal gambling, strip clubs, and prostitution flourished. Inevitably, payoffs to coppers followed, with Brisbane's top cop, Police Commissioner Terry Lewis, in central command of the systemic bribery.

The Fitzgerald inquiry into police corruption led to the end of 32 straight years of conservative government in Queensland and the rise of the Criminal Justice Commission, both events of 1989. The address of the CJC was for many years Creek St in the Brisbane CBD but the commission's grandkid, the CCC, moved into Fortitude Valley after it had gained a measure of respectability. The name

Fortitude did not honour strong drink but a ship which landed English free settlers there in 1849, 10 years before Queensland became independent of the Colony of New South Wales. Considering the links between Fortitude Valley, the Fitzgerald inquiry, the CJC, and the CCC, the Crime and Corruption Commission setting up residence in the suburb more commonly known as The Valley was a homecoming of sorts.

Moreton Futures Trust was the common link between witnesses at Operation Belcarra on day 3, Thursday April 20, 2017. The trust was a substantial donor to mayoral candidate Allan Sutherland in 2012 and 2016. Trustees John Ryan and Kirby Leeke were witnesses on day 3. Appearing as a witness between the pair was Allan Sutherland donor, Tim Connolly, who also had a hand in Moreton Futures Trust.

The first witness on day 3 was Dr John Alexander Ryan. The CCC presented as full a witness name as it could so people would not think it was America-based English equestrian John Saint Ryan appearing. Aspley GP Dr John Ryan said he was never involved in the administration of Moreton Futures Trust despite acknowledging his signature on the establishing trust deed of April 7, 2010.

Dr Ryan said he knew the other two signatories on the deed, Tim Connolly and Bryan Galvin, when the three were in a group called Friends of Pine Rivers.

'In the early 2000s, when there was a political committee set up to help fund applicants for council, but in the old Pine Rivers Shire Council,' Dr Ryan said.

'In a lead-up to the 2008 mayor elections, where the Pine Rivers was being amalgamated with Redcliffe and Caboolture into the Moreton Regional Council, and I was supporting Bryan Galvin, who was probably a 25- to 30-year friend and also my family solicitor for that period, and he was going against the present Mayor, Allan Sutherland, and other candidates for the Mayor position,' Dr Ryan said.

His memory may be astray because there is no record of Friends of Pine Rivers being active at the 2008 elections. If Friends of Pine Rivers did support Bryan Galvin for mayor, it must have done it discreetly and free of the public record. On a number of occasions I tried to confirm with the delegated holder of 2008 third-party disclosure forms, Moreton Bay Council, whether they had any records for Friends of Pine Rivers for 2004 and 2008 but the Council refused my requests for information. The CCC might have had more luck with such a request but I don't think they asked.

Dr Ryan said, 'I can't remember signing that (2010) deed (establishing Moreton Futures Trust), but I've subsequently found out from him (Mr Galvin) that he presented that to me in my surgery and that's where I signed it.'

One observer who attended all days of the Operation Belcarra hearing was Richard Firmin. Mr Firmin said the CCC persisted in an obvious oversight when the hearing saw witnesses take a nervous draught of water and then suffer memory loss. 'Why didn't they test that water?' Mr Firmin said to me. 'It looked like it was causing impaired memory for a lot of witnesses.'

Dr Ryan said he had recently found out about a change of trustee. 'What I understand is that in 2011, Bryan Galvin stepped down and apparently it did require two trustees, and Mr (Kirby) Leeke took his spot.'

He said it was only when police officers seconded by the CCC investigators came aknockin' that he knew what had been done in his name.

'I didn't know the Moreton (Futures) Trust existed until the (January 30, 2017) interview . . . and I certainly had no idea whether there was money in the trust.'

On December 22, 2015, I sent an email to Dr Ryan at Aspley Medical Centre asking him about Moreton Futures Trust and the transfer of more than $20,000 from Friends of Pine Rivers to Moreton Futures Trust in January, 2011. Dr Ryan made no acknowledgement of receiving my email.

Memory is an erratic beast at the best of times.

We journalists have an advantage over most people because we need only to remember what written records exist of events. I started working for the Pine Rivers Press in 2000, not long before Dr Ryan and anonymous mates set up Friends of Pine Rivers. My colleague Mike McAlary covered the rise of the Friends over the years but Dr Ryan would never tell Mike who his other mates were.

At the 2004 Pine Rivers Shire election, the last before amalgamation in 2008, Friends of Pine Rivers supported four councillors with gifts totalling $33,000.

CCC witness Cr Mike Charlton received $15,000 while the other three received $6000 each.

Deputy Mayor Bryan Galvin received no campaign funding as he was among five Councillors who had no opponents and were returned unopposed. My relations with some councillors deteriorated shortly after that when I wrote in my weekly humour column, *My Shout*, it was a shame the fortunate five had no opposition.

For years afterwards angry councillors would remind me of my negative comment which ignored the reality the councillors were returned unopposed because they were doing such a splendid job. It's funny how I had a markedly different interpretation. More recently a veteran Councillor told me the Council under Allan Sutherland was the best he had served on because there was no dissension. At the other end of the phone, I cringed.

Capping election spending may limit the campaign excesses of well supported incumbents and other candidates. But it does little to address the problem that some worthy potential candidates do not have access to the money to run an effective campaign.

By 2008, Advancing Moreton Leadership, tied to the Liberal Party, which later that year merged with the National Party, was supporting the campaign of

Mike Charlton and the mayoral campaign of Bryan Galvin. Mike Charlton won his division but Mr Galvin was defeated by former Mayor of Redcliffe City, Allan Sutherland. Redcliffe developers, brothers Bob and David Trask, gave $100,000 to Mr Sutherland's campaign.

What happened with Friends of Pine Rivers between 2004 and 2011 is something of a mystery but Moreton Futures Trustee Kirby Leeke told me Friends of Pine Rivers member Dr Ryan deposited $14,209.52 in Moreton Futures Trust on January 17, 2011. Mr Leeke told me Dr Ryan deposited $7724.58 in Moreton Futures Trust on January 18, 2011. Mr Leeke told me he assumed the money was transferred from Friends of Pine Rivers. It was a shame Dr Ryan could not assist the CCC hearing with any knowledge of the Moreton Futures Trust.

Transcript #1
Abridged by Bernie Dowling

Witness Dr John Ryan April 20, 2017
PO, Presiding Officer Alan MacSporran QC
CA, Counsel Assisting, Glen Rice QC
W, Witness Dr John Ryan
CCC hearing conducted at Fortitude Valley, Brisbane

CA I call Dr John Ryan. You are appearing here today in response to a notice to attend?
W Yes.

CA Dr Ryan are you aware of a trust called Moreton Futures Trust?
W I am, sir.
CA I'll show you a document. Just take a moment to have a look at that. Is that a copy of the deed of trust for the Moreton Futures Trust?
W I've recently understood it is, yes.
CA You will see it is dated 7 April 2010, Doctor?
W Yes.
CA It's your signature, is it not, amongst the signatures on the reverse page, on the second page?
W It is.
CA There are other parties named. Do you see on the top of the document the first name that's mentioned is that of Timothy Connolly? As at 7 April 2010, did you know Mr Connolly?
W I met him when I was interested in a private property subdivision in the 1990s. I probably met him socially before then and I met him subsequently in the context of Pine Rivers politics.
CA In what context did you meet him with respect to Pine Rivers politics?
W Well, the first is in the early 2000s, when there was a political committee set up to help fund applicants for the old Pine Rivers Shire Council.
CA Did that group have a name?
W The Pines – it did. Pines –
CA Friends of Pine Rivers – does that ring a bell?
W Friends of Pine Rivers. That's it, yes.
CA Was that an entity like this, that is to say, a trust, or did it have some structure?

W Well, I was invited to committees. I was not aware – I can't remember such a structure.

CA Okay. In relation to that entity, you mentioned that you went to meetings, committee meetings, I think you said?

W Well, the first time I became seriously involved is in a lead-up to the 2008 Mayor elections, where the Pine Rivers was being amalgamated with Redcliffe and Caboolture into the Moreton Regional Council, and I was supporting Bryan Galvin, who was probably a 25- to 30-year friend and also my family solicitor for that period, and he was going against the present Mayor, Allan Sutherland, and other candidates for the Mayor position.

(Dr Ryan's recollection might be wrong. It was at the 2004 Pine Rivers Shire Council when he was an active member of Friends of Pine Rivers. There is no record I am aware of that indicates Friends of Pine Rivers was a third party in 2008.)

CA Were you involved in choosing who would be supported financially from this group?

W Not in any way, no.

CA No? Was Mr Connolly involved in meetings such as you attended?

W Yes.

CA Do you know whether he was involved in fundraising for that group?

W Yes.

CA He was?

W Yes.

CA Organising?

W I wouldn't say – I can't remember who drove, you know, whatever. The things I remember is going to a group of four or five or six people and having an agenda and discussing the upcoming election.

CA Do you know who was responsible for actually disbursing money?

W I don't. I had no input how the money was disbursed, and I didn't do it.

CA Just getting back to the names we were speaking of, the other name that is on the trust deed is that of Bryan Galvin. Did you know him at the time this deed was signed?

W Well, I can't remember signing that deed, but I've subsequently found out from him that he presented that to me in my surgery and that's where I signed it.

CA Do you recollect that this was signed at your surgery?

W I cannot remember this document at all. I do not remember this document at all.

CA How did you know Mr Galvin as at April 2010?

W Well, I met him personally. I was practising medicine in Strathpine and Albany Creek and he was a solicitor with branches in The Valley and in Strathpine, and it was – actually, where I met him, we were both attending a Toastmasters – we joined a Toastmasters meeting – meetings in Strathpine together, so that was in the early 1980s, I'd say.

CA Were you friends?

W I'd say over the years, we became good friends. I don't see him that much, but I'd say we're good friends.

CA You mentioned earlier your involvement with Friends of Pine Rivers. Was Mr Galvin part of that group also?
W Well, you know, I'd – yes, very much so, yes.
CA Was he a beneficiary of funds of the group for the purpose of the 2008 election?
W Well, certainly in the latter part to where I was involved to 2008, with the council election – with the mayoral election, he was the major beneficiary, I would have thought, but I had no – I had no involvement in allocation of funding.
CA Yes.
W But he and Mike Charlton were the main drivers, I would have thought, and later on Kirby Leeke. But I wasn't involved in any of that distribution of funds or knowing which politician would get what.
CA You say that you can't recall signing this document. Looking at it now, do you agree that, as it reads, you accepted the role of acting as trustee?
W Well, that might be as it appears, but I thought I was out of politics of all sorts in 2008, and I do not recall signing that document and I did not know until very recently, when I had the interview by the policeman from here, that I was in any way involved after 2008, and that was a surprise to me.
CA Doctor, if you look on the first page under the heading "It is agreed as follows", you've actually agreed to a range of things, haven't you?
W I'm a suburban GP, not a lawyer, and I had my lawyer of 30 years asking me to sign it, and I'd had an involvement with him, and I signed it. It was

probably not the brightest thing in the world. I should have taken it home and studied it, but I didn't do that.

CA Did you receive a copy of this when it was signed – keep a copy, I mean?

W Well, it's not a very impressive-looking document. You know, it's two pages and it –

CA It has an impressive legal effect, doctor.

W Well, I'm not a lawyer, sir, but I can say that I almost certainly didn't keep a copy because I sign a lot of things that lawyers give – that lawyers and accountants give me and other people give me, and I perhaps place too much trust on the people looking after me, but there you go.

CA Can I ask you this: subsequent to your signing this in April 2010, did you carry out the role of trustee as described in this document?

W No.

CA Did you carry out any role?

W No.

CA Did you have anything to do with the operation of the Moreton Futures Trust – ?

W No.

CA – subsequent to signing this?

W No.

CA Did you at any stage authorise a disbursement of moneys held by the trust?

W No.

CA Do you know Kirby Leeke?

W I do.

CA Would you say, firstly, your background to knowing him? Where did you first meet him?
W Well, I met him in that Pines – the first time I actually remember him is not in early times, in the early 2000s, but leading up to Bryan Galvin's and – the first mayoral election for the amalgamated Moreton Shire, Moreton Region.
CA What was his occupation?
W Accountant.
CA In what capacity did you meet him?
W Well, he used to come to those meetings I referred to.
CA That's the Friends of Pine Rivers?
W Yes. Well, they were specifically – I'm just unclear. It's now – 2002 is now 13 (sic) years ago (in 2017), but the thing I do remember – his involvement in the several months leading up to the first Moreton election where I think he was fairly active in that.
CA In the context of the Friends of Pine Rivers or –
W Yes.
CA Did you know that in 2011 Mr Leeke replaced Bryan Galvin as a trustee of this Moreton Futures Trust?
W I only found that out in the last couple of weeks.
CA Subsequent to, if we make a point of demarcation being the 2008 elections, what contact have you had with Kirby Leeke since the 2008 council elections?
W Well, I think the last time I talked at any length with Kirby Leeke was on the night of the election, and he was doing a lot of statistics.

CA 2008?

W 2008. And I may have had one more conversation, and I've reflected upon this, and I don't think it had to do with that document. I think it had – well, it did have to do with that document in that I didn't know what it had – I didn't know about this document, so I didn't understand that – Quest Newspapers from Strathpine had rung me a couple of times asking to talk to me. They must have had a copy of this document. And I didn't return their call, but I may have talked to Kirby once since 2008 about that Quest inquiry because I didn't know what it was all about and I thought he might.

CA Is that in recent times?

W Oh, no, that would be three or four years ago.

(It had to be no further back than 12-16 months because I was the Quest reporter asking the questions in late 2015, early 2016.)

CA Did you know that Kirby Leeke had a connection of some kind with the Moreton Futures Trust?

W I found out – yes. Well, I found out subsequent to Bryan Galvin stepping down in 2011, he stepped in as my fellow trustee.

CA When did you find that out?

W Last week.

CA Did you have anything to do with the opening of a National Australia Bank account in your name as trustee for the Moreton Futures Trust?

W Oh, dear. The only thing that has been explained to me is by the policeman, in that this 2010 deed was to enable funds left over from Pines to morph into the expanded Moreton thing. Now, unless I signed something with Bryan Galvin to that effect on the same day, I don't know. But would my signing that two-page document empower that?

CA There are bank statements. There may not be much point in showing them to you because you say you have no knowledge of the accounts or their operation; is that so?

W I've never signed a cheque right throughout since – this century, I haven't signed a cheque or transferred money or allocated funds in any way, ever.

(Dr Ryan transferred $14,209.52 from Friends of Pine Rivers to Moreton Futures Trust on January 17, 2011, and $7724.58 from Friends of Pine Rivers to Moreton Futures Trust on January 18, 2011.)

CA I take it, then, that you would know nothing about the use of those accounts for the funding of Mayor Sutherland's campaign for the 2016 elections?

W I've had no knowledge of funding activities this century in either the Pines or that and never signed a cheque, never operated an account, never known who was going to get the money, never allocated it to any councillors. I have not been involved financially whatsoever.

CA That's the evidence, Mr Commissioner.

5

THE NEXT WITNESS was town planner Tim Connolly who agreed he was a signatory to the 2010 Moreton Futures trust deed as a 'settlor'. Town planners are essential people in the development industry, working for developers and councils, and sometimes both, though usually not at the same time.

'I think I was just a convenient person at the time,' Mr Connolly said. 'I had something to do with the 2008 election for Bryan Galvin.'

The town planner's inspection of the document lead to this exchange between Mr Connolly (W) and Mr Rice (CA.)

W This is the first time I've seen that signed (2010) document.

CA Well, presumably you saw it when you signed it?

W I saw that bit, but I haven't seen the rest of it.

Mr Connolly said he attended a Moreton Futures Trust fundraiser at Lakeside motor raceway and a dinner in 2010 and invited friends to it but had no involvement after that.

'I participated in some fundraising events, yes, around that 2010, but not since that time.

'I didn't organise those events.'

Mr Connolly said he had no involvement with Friends of Pine Rivers.

No Midas School of Alchemy exists where property developers learn to turn marginal riverside scrub into banks of gold. A truckload of skills are needed after evicting plants and animals, often with extreme prejudice, to turn land into a housing or other commercial development. You will need, in a roughly chronological order, a project strategist, finance broker, accountant, lawyer, project manager, and town planners. That's just to have your project ready for judgement by the local council. You haven't clipped a blade of grass, yet.

You would think Einstein would struggle putting that sort of stuff together but the developers I have met are no geniuses.

Developer Chazza had a sports entertainment business which he sold to take early retirement in his 50s. He had a reasonably large block of land near his business and he paid someone to build four townhouses on it. He was not impressed with the way the builder went about the process and decided he could do better. Starting small, he created a family business of commercial development.

Chazza told me when he was starting out he went to see Mayor Leonowens – pronounced Leon-owens – to say he wanted to build an adult shop as he thought he might get into that business. God-fearing Christian Ms Leonowens said Chazza could go right ahead but he would never build as much as a chook shed in the area after that. The Mayor was as much responsible as anyone for Chazza's success as he pursued the creation of commercial enterprises other than adult shops.

Another developer Pip learned the development ropes as a land broker. He would facilitate the sale of farm land to developers. The southern boundary of Pine Rivers Shire is only 25 kilometres from Brisbane CBD but it was a rural area until the late 1960s. As the area moved from rural to provincial to suburban it provided lots of opportunities to buy land to sub-divide for housing.

One developer Nifty took young land broker Pip under his wing and taught him what the business was all about.

When I first met Pip his humility and friendliness impressed me but I was disconcerted how he conveyed to me from the get-go he was a committed Christian. Australians by and large keep their religious inclinations to themselves but I came to notice in Pine Rivers groups of business people united in their love of the Lord, right-wing politics, and making money. I have only a superficial understanding of the interconnections and how they play out. No one invited me to join the holy mates' club.

From my viewpoint your average successful developer is an ordinary person, usually a man, who started small while learning the trade and meeting the right people.

I wouldn't like you to think that I am on personal terms with every developer in the Pine Rivers district of the Moreton Bay Region. I was a reporter with the Pine Rivers Press for 17 years so I got to know some of the local developers. Others have HQs in Brisbane and on the Sunshine or Gold Coast, or interstate. They don't want to engage me in conversation because my main interest would be in how their development would affect the lives and health of the community. That effect is not always benign.

When a development application is presented to council, the name of the developer might be in one line of a long document. Sometimes you might have trouble finding out the name of the parent company, let alone any of the directors. The Operation Belcarra report has recommended new development applications contain names and addresses of directors and any political donations.

At the moment most applications are lodged by town planners. Socrates said, 'By far the greatest and most admirable form of wisdom is that needed to plan and beautify cities and human communities.' The great thinker did not predict the advent of the modern town planner.

Transcript #2
Abridged by Bernie Dowling

Witness Tim Connolly April 20, 2017
PO, Presiding Officer Alan MacSporran QC
CA, Counsel Assisting, Glen Rice QC

W, Witness Tim Connolly
CCC hearing conducted at Fortitude Valley, Brisbane
CA Commissioner, I call Timothy Joseph Connolly.
CA Mr Connolly, you're a town planner by occupation; is that right?
W That's right, yes.
CA How long have you been a town planner?
W Thirty-five years.
CA You've done town planning work, have you, in the Moreton Bay region?
W Well, I do work in the Moreton Bay region as well as other councils.
CA Have you worked in Pine Rivers?
W Pine Rivers, correct.
CA And Redcliffe?
W When they were existing, yes.
CA Caboolture?
W Yes.
CA You have, or at least your employer has, clients from the private sector?
W Correct.
CA And public sector also?
W I believe so, yes.
CA And your employer's clients include property developers?
W Yes.
CA I want to ask you whether you're familiar with an entity known as the Moreton Futures Trust?
W Yes, I am.
CA Can I show you a copy of a trust deed, which is Exhibit 45, Commissioner.

CA It will come up on the screen, but I'll show you the document also. Do you recognise that trust deed?
W Yes.
CA Did you sign that on the reverse page?
W Yes, I have.
CA In the capacity of settlor of the trust?
W Yes, that's my understanding.

(I know you are dying to ask. A settlor places assets under the control of the trustees for the benefit of the beneficiaries.)

CA It's dated 7 April 2010. Is that the date that you signed it?
W That's my recollection, yes.
CA There are some other persons named on the document. I will just ask you, firstly, what your involvement was with them. Dr John Ryan, did you know him as at April 2010?
W Yes, I would have. Yes, definitely.
CA What's the background to that?
W Originally as a client, and I suppose he's a friend, yes.
CA What about Bryan Galvin, what did you know of him at April 2010?
W I originally met him as a solicitor, as a businessman in the council, or in the region that I worked, and then I think he later became a councillor and he also ran for Mayor in 2008.
CA Before I ask you more about that, do you know of a group, or perhaps it is a trust, called Friends of Pine Rivers or a name of that kind?
W Yes, I have a recollection of that around –

CA Did you have any involvement with the operation of that group?
W No.
CA Do you know what its purpose was?
W I think its purpose was to raise funds.
CA For what purpose?
W For elections.
CA Could you explain, then, how you came to be settlor of the trust and signed this document?
W I think I was just a convenient person at the time.
CA It's unlikely you were roped in off the street, is it, Mr Connolly?
W I had something to do with the 2008 election for Bryan Galvin.
CA The witnesses to the various signatures are all different persons; correct?
W It looks like that, yes.
CA That suggests that the document wasn't signed all at the one time?
W I don't know what it suggests, mate.
CA Well, do you have any recollection of – .
W This is the first time I've seen that signed document.
CA Well, presumably you saw it when you signed it?
W I saw that bit, but I haven't seen the rest of it.
CA After the trust was formed in April 2010, did you have any involvement in its operation?
W No, I had no influence.
CA No, but insofar as one of the objects was to hold money and disburse it, first of all, money has to be

raised. I'm asking you if you had any involvement in raising any money for the purpose of this trust.
W I participated in some fundraising events, yes, around that 2010, but not since that time.
CA What events do you recall?
W I recall there was a race day at Lakeside and a dinner.
CA Were you there in any capacity beyond being an attendee?
W I attended and invited some of my friends.
CA You don't know what role Dr John Ryan had?
W He was the trustee.
CA Do you know Kirby Leeke?
W I do.
CA How do you know him?
W He was an objector to a development that I was a consultant on.
CA His name doesn't appear on the trust deed, does it?
W No.
CA Did you know that he became a substitute trustee for Bryan Galvin?
W I was aware of that.
CA Do you know anything about how any money of the trust might have been applied towards Mayor Sutherland's campaign fund?
W No, no knowledge of that.
CA Thanks, Mr Connolly.
PO Thank you. Thank you, Mr Connolly, for coming. You are excused.

6

THE ARGUMENT for allowing third parties to collect donations and pass them on to political candidates is somewhat compelling.

The idea is that good corporate citizens can exercise support for a type of candidate rather than a particular candidate. In the case of a trade union, it might give money to a Labor Party fund to pass on to someone tolerant of unionism. In the case of businesspeople they might wish to express their view conservatives make better money managers. Unions and businesses are happy to let knowledgeable people make the call on the appropriate candidates to support. Trustee Kirby Leeke told me the Moreton Futures Trust was set up to support talented candidates of a conservative bent.

The fact almost all of the collection went to the Mayor Allan Sutherland in 2016 and 2012 (more than $200,000 in total) came from the considered judgement of trustees Kirby Leeke and John Ryan though Dr Ryan denied having made any contribution to the selection.

The problem was that Councillor Sutherland was not compelled to find out the people, mostly developers and those in allied industries, who supported Moreton Futures Trust. Cr Sutherland was compelled by law to know who the trustees were but he failed in this regard. He did not know he had to do it, he told the CCC.

It is a pity the architects of the prevailing electoral laws did not foresee the messy situation allowing third parties would create. They could have obligated political beneficiaries to know who gave them money through a trust. Maybe it is the arrogance of hindsight, but I would have thought that was rather obvious.

The third witness on April 20 was accountant and Moreton Futures Trustee, Kirby Leeke. He replaced Bryan Galvin as a trustee in 2011.

Mr Leeke said he was not part of Friends of Pine Rivers. 'I had heard of it. I wasn't part – I attended meetings when they met occasionally.'

Dr John Ryan told my colleague Mike McAlary in 2004 that Friends of Pine Rivers was nothing but an informal group who met to discuss good governance. Maybe Mr Leeke was a member without being aware of it.

Kirby Leeke only learned of the existence of Moreton Futures Trust sometime after it had been formed. 'At that point in time (during 2010 or 2011), I believed it was to establish and promote Bryan Galvin as a candidate for Mayor (of Moreton Bay Region.)

'We used to have meetings at Bryan Galvin's office,' Mr Leeke said. 'I think Tim Connolly would be at some of the meetings. I think John Ryan might have been at some of those meetings as well.'

Mr Galvin decided not to run in 2012. 'I think he decided – once he decided not to contest the 2012 election, he didn't want to continue as a trustee,' Mr Leeke said. 'He asked me if I would, and I agreed to accept the nomination or the position.

'At that point in time we decided we'd support Councillor Allan Sutherland.'

Cr Sutherland won and at some time in 2013 a group met at Albany Creek to discuss his re-election in 2016.

'It would be – probably somewhere in the 2013 year, it became evident that he (Allan Sutherland) was proposing to run.

'We used to have a Coffee Club meeting,' Mr Leeke said. 'It wasn't a formal meeting. And various people would be at different times – Tim Connolly, myself, Bryan Galvin. There was another gentleman by the name of John (Tetley) who is the lessee of Lakeside, would come along. I can't remember his surname. I think Mike Charlton might have come along once or twice as well.'

Yet it was not until late January 2016 that Allan Sutherland declared he would run.

Earlier in January 2016 Mr Leeke emailed two Quest journalists, 'The reason we have not chosen to support Allan for the 2016 election yet is we are aware of possible alternate candidates.'

In his email, he was not completely frank with me and my colleague, Walter Burns. 'At this point in time we had probably decided to support Allan

Sutherland,' Mr Leeke told the CCC. 'But I wasn't going to tell the journos that.'

Transcript #3
Abridged by Bernie Dowling

Witness Kirby Leeke April 20, 2017
PO, Presiding Officer Alan MacSporran QC
CA, Counsel Assisting, Glen Rice QC
W, Witness Kirby Leeke
CA Commissioner, I'm in a position to call Mr Kirby James Leeke.
PO Thank you. Mr Leeke, are you happy to take the oath?
W I am.
CA Mr Leeke, you're an accountant by occupation?
W I am.
CA Mr Leeke, are you aware of a trust fund called Moreton Futures Trust?
W I am.
CA I'll just show you a copy of the trust deed. If we could see Exhibit 45.
W I think I probably provided the Commission with the copy in the first place.
CA Well, you may have done.
PO We're eternally grateful, Mr Leeke.
    (Reading Mr MacSporran's interjection always brings a smile)
CA You notice the date on it is the date of formation of the trust, which was the 7th of April 2010. Did you know at that time that that trust was to be formed?

W I did not know.
CA When did you first learn of the trust's existence?
W Look, somewhere in that 2010/2011 period, but I wasn't part of the establishment of it.
CA You had had some association with a prior trust, it may have been, by a name I think of Friends of Pine Rivers. Does that ring a bell?
W I was involved in the campaign. I've been involved in campaigns in the Pine Rivers – well, what was the Pine Rivers, of course, for probably fifteen, twenty years. I had heard of it. I wasn't part – I attended meetings when they met occasionally. I didn't attend every one of their meetings. I didn't actually even know they had a bank account, but I knew of – I knew of the existence of Friends of Pine Rivers, yes.
CA Knew of it as what, just a group of people, or did you know of any formal structure?
W I did not know of the structure of it at the time, no.
CA You attended some meetings of persons connected with it?
W They were more campaign type meetings, yes.
CA Campaign for what?
W At the time we were working with Bryan Galvin for –
CA Towards what election?
W Towards the 2008 election, I believe.
   (Again, I have seen no record of Friends of Pine Rivers being a third party in 2008.)
CA That would be the amalgamation one, so it would be memorable for that reason?

CA What was the object of the group, I'll call it a group, Friends of Pine Rivers?
W   We were supporting Bryan Galvin as the candidate for Mayor.
CA Was there money raised through Friends of Pine Rivers for Bryan Galvin's campaign?
W I believe so, yes.
CA And spent on his campaign?
W I believe so, yes.
CA You will see on that (Moreton Futures) trust deed there are a number of names, not including yours, but as at April 2010 did you know, for example, Timothy Connolly?
W I did.
CA Well, obviously you did know Bryan Galvin?
W Yes, I did.
CA What was your background to your association with him?
W I first met him when he was elected as a councillor for the Pine Rivers Shire Council and from there – that was the first time I think I met him. And that would be fifteen, twenty years ago or thereabouts.
CA Mr Galvin didn't contest the 2012 election, did he?
W He did not, no. But we believed, until about six months before the election, that he was going to be – you know, we were working, campaigning towards his nominating and running for election.
CA Was that the reason for your involvement in the trust –
W It was.

CA --to see him re-elected?

(Bryan Galvin was not up for re-election in 2012 as he lost to Allan Sutherland in 2008.)

W Correct, yes.

CA But he ended up not running?

W Correct.

CA Who else, apart from yourself, was involved leading up to the 2012 election in raising money for the purpose of his re-election?

W I have to – I honestly can't remember. We used to have meetings at Bryan Galvin's office which, at that point in time, was near the Westfield Shopping Centre in Strathpine. There were different people there, including Bryan's secretary, but I don't think she had much to do with it. I think Tim Connolly would be at some of the meetings. I think John Ryan might have been at some of those meetings as well.

CA You became a trustee of the trust, didn't you?

W I did.

CA How did you come to be a replacement trustee for Bryan Galvin?

W Bryan asked me to be. I think he decided – once he decided not to contest the 2012 election, he didn't want to continue as a trustee. I had been doing the paperwork, as in the accounting work, behind the scene. He asked me if I would, and I agreed to accept the nomination or the position.

CA In doing so, you became responsible for the carrying out of the terms of the trust; correct?

W I did.

CA Mr Galvin, not in the end having contested the 2012 election, was another candidate supported by Moreton Futures Trust?
W At that point in time we decided we'd support Councillor Allan Sutherland, yes.
CA He was running for Mayor?
W He was.
CA And was elected?
W He was.
CA When you say "we decided" to support Allan Sutherland, who do you mean?
W Probably Bryan Galvin, myself, I think Tim Connolly may have been involved in that decision. We didn't have a formal meeting. We probably had a meeting in literally The Coffee Club at Albany Creek, and we had raised the money. We were doing work, what were we going to do with it, so we decided to support Allan Sutherland.

(Over coffee, we gave away $100,000 to a stranger.)

CA Did you, being the accountant, have the bookkeeping responsibilities for the management of the money?
W From about two months prior to my taking over as the trustee I did, yes.
CA From the time of opening this account, there being only two signatories, which of you operated on the accounts?
W I did.
CA To the exclusion of Dr Ryan?
W Predominantly, yes.

CA Moving forward towards the 2016 elections, was there any fundraising towards that election?
W There was initially. In either late 2012 or early 2013, there were a lot of rumours floating around, and they were rumours that Councillor Sutherland would not recontest the mayoral position at the 2016 election, so we were trying to think of how we would fund and support a potential candidate for the mayoral position, if Councillor Sutherland didn't nominate. A bit like we did with Bryan Galvin in the previous election.
CA At some point was a decision made to support Mayor Sutherland?
W It would be – probably somewhere in the 2013 year, it became evident that he was proposing to run.
CA When you speak of "we", can you tell us again who you're speaking of?
W Oh, there was myself. We used to have a Coffee Club meeting – a meeting is a collection of two people. It wasn't a formal meeting. We didn't have minutes. We didn't have – et cetera. And various people would be at different times – Tim Connolly, myself, Bryan Galvin. There was another gentleman by the name of John (Tetley), who is the lessee of Lakeside, would come along. I can't remember his surname. I think Mike Charlton might have come along once or twice as well. It was a loose collection of people.
CA When you were spoken to, I think, by investigators, you might have used the expression "committee" or "committee meetings". Is that the

kind of thing that you were referring to, what's in fact The Coffee Club meetings?

W It was, yes. The only meetings we ever had were at The Coffee Club.

CA With what regularity?

W In 2013, we were trying to have them probably monthly. They probably didn't happen monthly. They ended up being cancelled and probably be two-monthly. But towards the end of that period – we haven't had – honestly haven't had a meeting in three years, probably, four years, you know, like - after it became evident that Councillor Sutherland was going to continue, we did not continue having the meetings, because we didn't think we would have to try and get another candidate and try and get his profile up.

(The timeline of these meetings, as outlined by Kirby Leeke, above, is confusing. Three to four years after the second half of 2013 means there were no meetings before the 2016 election of March 19.)

CA Was Dr Ryan an attendee at any of these Coffee Club meetings?

W He was a couple of times, yes.

CA Was he involved in a decision to support Councillor Sutherland?

W The suggestion – we did not make a conscious decision. It was a thing that evolved on us over a period of time, if I can put it that way. We didn't say, "Okay, we're going to have a vote", and three people for, one against, or anything along those lines. It evolved over that time. He was probably at one of those meetings while we were discussing it, yes.

CA On this subject, you wrote an email, I think, in January this year (2016) to a couple of, look like journalists?(Me and Walter Burns.)

W I had someone driving me insane from the Redcliffe local rag, yes. I thought it was before January, to be honest, but, yes, that was going on in –

CA Just have a look, then, at this email. Is that an email that you wrote on the 21st of January this year (2016)?

W I believe so, yes.

CA Who was it addressed to?

W A Mr Bernie Dowling who, I believe, is an editor of the paper over there.

(Not the editor, just a humble reporter on the *Pine Rivers Press*, the sister paper of the *Redcliffe and Bayside Herald*.)

CA Which paper?

W I don't know. The local rag. Is it Murdoch press? Whoever's got the local rag on the Redcliffe Peninsula.

(For 17 years, I wrote for the *Pine Rivers Press*. Both papers are ultimately owned by News Corp. I always winced when someone called the newspaper I wrote for a 'rag' though I suppose you could say it was a metaphor for cleaning up messes or producing a sprightly jazz tune.)

CA There's a cc to another person from the same organisation?

W Correct.
CA Also perhaps a journalist, do you know?
W I believe that he was. They were both ringing me, they were both asking me different questions at different times, and they were stepping on each other's toes and, you know, duplicating questions and everything.
CA They were asking you quite a range of details, I suggest, about Moreton Futures Trust?
W They were.
CA This is at least one response to them?
W Mmm-hmm.
CA I tender that email.
PO Exhibit 53.
CA Is what you explained in that email correct, that is to say, that the trust was formed to support Bryan Galvin as mayoral candidate for 2012?
W Yes, and I've previously said that today, yes.
CA And the early fundraising was done to support Bryan; correct?
W Correct.
CA Then when he made a decision not to contest 2012, you go on to say, "We, John and I, decided to support Allan Sutherland." Is that the situation?
W Predominantly, yes.
CA That it was your decision and Dr John Ryan's decision to support Allan Sutherland?
W It was, but Bryan Galvin was involved in the discussion. Again, it wasn't a vote with just the two of us. There were other people we discussed at the time, yes.

(In 2008, Mr Galvin, a former Deputy Mayor of Pine Rivers, stood against Cr Sutherland, a former Mayor of Redcliffe. Both Pine Rivers and Redcliffe Councils were against amalgamation into Moreton Bay Region. But a bitter feud erupted when Councillor Sutherland suggested, instead of amalgamation, Pine Rivers give to Redcliffe all the territory east of the Bruce Highway. This would include the developing areas of North Lakes, Mango Hill, and Griffin, mostly consisting of closely settled small blocks, a rates bonanza for the local council.

Obviously Mr Galvin did not hold a grudge after his 2008 defeat. Similarly, Mike Charlton, another previous foe of Councillor Sutherland, was won over by the charms of the Redcliffe conqueror of Moreton Bay Region.)

CA Okay. In the third paragraph (of the email to me and Walter Burns), you say, "The reason we have not chosen to support Allan for the 2016 election yet is we are aware of possible alternate candidates." Does that convey that as at January 2016, you still hadn't made a decision whether Councillor Sutherland would be supported or not?

W We were very suspicious that we would be supporting him, but we did not know if there was anyone else that we may – and Bryan Galvin may have even come along and said he wanted to run.

CA That's not too long before the election, only less than two months. At what – well, was a decision made to support Allan Sutherland?

W I would honestly say at this point in time we had probably decided to support Allan Sutherland, but I wasn't going to tell the journos that.

(Moreton Futures Trust was formed to promote good governance which obviously does not preclude the sport of misleading the media.)

CA Did you have any role in soliciting any donations from any donors?

W No, I did not. I did not.

CA Were you aware of the money going in?

W I had daily online access to the account, so I checked the account daily and would transfer money out into the online saver account to get interest on it, yes.

CA You mentioned that it evolved, I think was your word, that Councillor Sutherland would in fact be supported financially. Did you have any direct communication with him to that effect?

W I spoke to Allan Sutherland once at a function that was Brian Battersby's farewell. He had served 42 years as a councillor. I spoke to Allan there. He did ask me if we would be supporting him and I did say yes, but I think that was the only time I spoke to Allan in the 12 months before the election – well, during – pardon me, during the term of the election.

CA Was any part of that conversation to do with the extent to which he might be supported? Was there any talk of dollar figures, for example?

W There was none.

CA It was left on a fairly general basis?

W   Correct. Most – honestly, most of our conversation was about those two journos who'd been driving me insane.

CA Did you pay any invoice in respect of any other candidate's expenses?

W No.

CA What was the origin of this sheet that you wrote on?

W Somebody dropped a cheque in to my office. I think it was for $20,000. I think the person who dropped it in was a (developer) David Trask and that's why I've written "David" there, and that was the details that I could track down for where it came from.

CA A sheet of paper with a $20,000 cheque?

W   With the cheque that said "Moreton Futures Trust".

CA No prior warning?

W No.

CA No call, "Kirby, I'm coming in", et cetera?

W None at all, sir.

CA Did that surprise you?

W It has happened before.

Timeline Trouble

As one of those two journos driving Mr Leeke insane, I would like to defend myself. Maybe I was trying to work out the timeline of his recollections of Moreton Futures Trust and the support for Allan Sutherland at the March 19, 2016, council election. Councillor

Sutherland declared himself as a candidate on January 26, 2016.

CA At some point was a decision made to support Mayor Sutherland?
W It would be – probably somewhere in the 2013 year . . .

But as of January 21, 2016, before the March election of that year, Mr Leeke was telling me and the CCC hearing it was not certain Moreton Futures Trust would support Allan Sutherland.

CA Does that [email] convey that as at January 2016, you still hadn't made a decision whether Councillor Sutherland would be supported or not?
W We were very suspicious that we would be supporting him, but we did not know if there was anyone else that we may – and Bryan Galvin may have even come along and said he wanted to run.

Mr Leeke tweaks his evidence about his disposition on January 21, 2016.

W I would honestly say at this point in time we had probably decided to support Allan Sutherland, but I wasn't going to tell the journos that.

No, you would not want to tell that to journos inquiring into public disclosure of political donations.

7

THIRD PARTY SUPPORT of a candidate for public office can be a love affair from afar, a bit like a fan's infatuation with a Hollywood movie star.

Moreton Futures Trust was unincorporated which meant the trustees and the financially anointed should have known each other. The politician did not need to know the donors to the trust but it would seem common sense for the recipient of largesse to know who gave, in case a donor later had a matter before council which the receiver might accidentally vote on when they could otherwise declare a perceived conflict of interest.

You might wonder why a politician would not inspect who donated to a third party when the donations became a matter of public record. Yet strange things happen in politics. And perhaps it would be better if we, the public, had a more charitable view of our elected representatives. That seems to be the opinion of Greg Hallam, CEO of the Local Government Association of Queensland, an organisation which has been representing councils and sitting councillors for a long time.

The Local Government Association of Queensland was established in 1896 and, by 2017, Greg Hallam had been its CEO for 25 years.

Council assisting the inquiry Glen Rice and Witness Mr Hallam discussed his official longevity.

CA That's a position that you have held since 1992?
W Yes, almost 25 years.
CA A long time.
W Indeed.

Mr Hallam said the LGAQ's mission was to strengthen the ability and performance of local government to better serve the community. Actually he said more than that in a sentence which contained about 80 words but working for the community came first ahead of working for its 77 member councils.

'We take that the Mayor and/or the CEO are representing the view of the governing mind,' Mr Hallam said. The Council CEO and the mayor were paragons of the herrschenden Geist, Mr Hallam, if he had chosen to wax even more philosophical, might have said. But councillors are mum-and-dad politicians, as Mr Hallam would remind us later. Mum-and-dad pollies do not have German metaphysics for breakfast with their coffee and Vegemite on toast.

The LGAQ is in the process of adding a new skill to its duties which currently include much back-room administrative work for councils.

'We're still in the process of investigating establishing an independent electoral monitor,' Mr Hallam said. 'That's to look at questions of, in the current common parlance, fake news, so people making all sorts of accusations and allegations in respect of the wrongdoings of councillors . . .'

Council assisting, Mr Rice, asked, 'What use are you going to make of the information you get?'

'We would hope that by creating such a role, the simple creation may stop some persons from abusing the good name of sitting councillors unfairly,' Mr Hallam said.

On the question of reforming the process of transparency of council elections, the LGA has a mixture of views from the progressive to the laissez-faire and agnostic.

'We support real-time disclosures up to seven days before the election, and then we say that no further donations should be received for that election,' Mr Hallam said.

Why select seven days Mr Rice asked. Biblical, Mr Hallam replied.

'We see no real reason why the returns to the ECQ should take 15 weeks,' Mr Hallam said. 'We think it could be as few as 30 days.'

In relation to the completion of the Councillors' register of interests and gifts register, the LGAQ believes they should be completed before they take office.

The association supports the (crazy, IMO) idea that all candidates complete a register of interests and associations before an election. The register of interests includes the financial and other interests of the elected member and it includes membership of political parties.

Mr Hallam offered an excellent definition of good public policy as 'one that you can enforce and one that improves the system.'

Much of the problems of electoral disclosure law is the lack of resources to enforce. The cynic might say there is a concomitant lack of will to enforce. When the lack of enforcement is exposed, the tendency is for an administration to cry 'under-resourced'. It is important, as Mr Hallam said, to be able to enforce. Why then would you broaden the interests register to the mass of unelected candidates, making reliable audits impossible?

Greg Hallam is not reflecting my experience of councils when he says, 'I mean, as an old veteran of 30-odd years in local government, we go through these swings where we are either pro-development or anti-development, and there is a cycle and you see it. Probably the cycle comes around more often now than it did years ago.'

The two councils I have observed over the past 20 or so years did not swing on the moral pendulum of pro and anti-development. I have never come across a councillor let alone a council I would describe as anti-development.

A veteran Brisbane journalist, Roger Davis, recently called on the State Government to overrule the democratic process and get rid of the Toowoomba council because the well exposed journo considered the council anti-development.

Shortly after I became a reporter for the Pine Rivers Press I spoke with one councillor who was a member of the local koala protection association. We were discussing whether council should prosecute a land owner who had cut down two protected koala fodder trees to build a swimming pool.

The councillor/ koala protector became irate. 'Don't you think someone has the right to cut down gum trees for a swimming pool,' he asked.

'No, I don't,' I replied calmly.

Exasperated, the Councillor could not believe my reply and repeated the question more loudly.

Transcript #4
Abridged by Bernie Dowling

Witness Greg Hallam April 27, 2017
PO, Presiding Officer Alan MacSporran QC
CA, Counsel Assisting, Glen Rice QC
W, Witness Greg Hallam

CA Commissioner, I call Mr Gregory Hallam.
CA Mr Hallam, you're the Chief Executive Officer of the Local Government Association of Queensland; am I right?
W That's correct.
CA That's a position that you have held since 1992?
W Yes, almost 25 years.
CA A long time.
W Indeed.

CA Could you explain, to begin with, Mr Hallam, what the role of the Local Government Association is?

W Yes, thank you. The Local Government Association was established in 1896. Our mission is to strengthen the ability and performance of local government to better serve the community, and our objects are to promote the interests, rights and entitlements of its members, improve the efficient performance of local government in Queensland, advise and counsel members – I should say "member" in that instance is the body corporate; it is the governing mind of the council, not individuals - in matters of doubt or difficulty, monitor and take action in relation to any legislation affecting members and undertake and promote actions endorsed by our annual conference at policy executive and board.

CA Your membership, then, consists of?

W Seventy-seven councils of Queensland. We are a voluntary body, but all 77 councils are members.

CA Being, I think you said, the bodies corporate of those councils?

W Yes, the bodies corporate. We take that the Mayor and/or the CEO are representing the view of the governing mind.

CA You referred to your outward-bound calling processes? Perhaps you might explain in a bit more detail what that consists of? Firstly, it is obviously forming a relationship with those folks. "Those folks" being?

W Sorry, my apology. The 500-odd councillors of Queensland. The LGAQ is an extensive business as well. Our group total turnover is around about a billion dollars a year. So we own and operate an insurance company, not a brokerage but a full suite – a full suite of services, I should say; a workers' comp (compensation, accident insurance, compulsory for employers in Australia) licence to most councils in Queensland; a procurement function, Local Buy; a shared services and facilities management company, Propel; and an infrastructure delivery group, LGIS.

CA This hearing is more focused on the electoral process. Is there any training or education provided to councillors in respect of, for example, obligations under the Local Government Electoral Act?

W No, not as such. We see that as the province of the Electoral Commission of Queensland and the Department of Local Government. But we do give advice from time to time for sitting councillors, obviously. If they ask a question, we would answer to the best of our ability.

CA You mentioned that you don't have any formal role in the electoral process, but do you find, as a matter of practice, that in the course of election campaigns you tend to field inquiries from councillors about how to deal with issues that arise in the course of a campaign?

W To be honest, not a lot during the conduct of elections. The sort of stuff that we would get are people crying foul about potential defamations, abuse of the political process, matters referred to the Commission. But, no, we don't get many questions, certainly I don't, about the actual ins and outs of the Local Government Electoral Act.

CA It sounds like you field complaints, though?

W Many, many complaints.

CA On what kinds of topics, Mr Hallam?

W People would attack the good name of a candidate. They would allege that they have referred matters to this Commission, the Ombudsman, the Auditor General and any number of watchdogs. Very false submissions have been made about the powers of councils, that they can do certain things when they can't, or the financial position of councils. We're still in the process of investigating establishing an independent electoral monitor. That's to look at questions of, in the current common parlance, fake news, so people making all sorts of accusations and allegations in respect of the wrongdoings of councillors.

CA You mentioned the electoral monitor. Is that an existing position or a foreshadowed position?

W Foreshadowed. Because of the abuse, in our mind, the abuse of the system against sitting councillors, and we're on the record as saying it's the worst in living memory.

CA In terms of complaints that you have received?

W It was quite pernicious, and a lot of it involved not the mainstream media but the use of social media. So we've got a project under way at the minute exploring at least the possibility to have someone, not with judicial powers, obviously, or extra-judicial powers, but an ability to have a senior person, supported by appropriate research and media-monitoring systems, that could call in quick time the straight-out fake news and furphies.

(Is this 'senior' an Australian Donald-Trump Doppelganger, able to take the mouse finger to Twitter to abruptly and accurately declare fake news?)

CA What use are you going to make of the information you get?

W We would hope that by creating such a role, the simple creation may stop some persons from abusing the good name of sitting councillors unfairly.

CA In response to an invitation, I think the association has made a submission to the Commission for the purpose of this hearing?

W Yes, correct.

CA There were a couple of issues specifically touched on in that submission, Mr Hallam. One was to do with disclosure of electoral donations. You would be aware, I think, under the Local Government Electoral Act, of the disclosure regime as it exists?

W Yes.

CA And that it requires disclosure returns and they may be submitted up to 15 weeks after polling date. Do you and your association have a view about the adequacy of that kind of a regime in giving electors information that they might be assisted by in placing their vote?

W We do. In the first instance, we've supported real-time disclosures. So we support real-time disclosures up to seven days before the election, and then we say that no further donations should be received for that election.

CA Why select seven days?

W Biblical.

(Biblical? As in the *Bible* or Samuel L. Jackson from the movie *Pulp Fiction*? 'And I will execute great vengeance upon them with furious rebukes..')

CA Does the association, then, support the government's decision to introduce real-time disclosure in the Bill that is, I think, presently going through the House?

W We do. We do, and then we go beyond that and say this, that in relation to the completion of the members' register of interests and gifts register, they must be completed before they take office.

CA That's the second issue that you raised in your submission.

W Yes. As it currently stands, it is 30 days, so there is a potential for councils to sit and determine matters without those registers being completed. We say now that the best practice would be for all registers to be completed before people can take up their position at a council meeting.

CA Just enlighten us as to what is the content of the register of interests?

W The register of interests goes to a number of things: the financial and other interests of the elected member and their wife, although it's (the spouse's) held in private; it details any interests that might affect the conduct of their business; it goes to the membership of political parties. It covers off on a range of things, but it is separate from the gifts register, which is the register in which they must lodge the particulars of political donations.

CA One matter that a couple of councillors have raised in the course of hearing in this session is that the register of interests is not applicable to new candidates, and some councillors feel it is not a level playing field.

W Our submission is that they should.

CA Would a register of interests, if it were extended to new candidates and not only limited to councillors, expose political affiliations, memberships and so forth?

W Yes. Yes, it would.

CA At what level does it operate? What kind of information of that type currently is disclosed by councillors?

W You simply have to record, if you are a member of a political party, what that party is. A political party or a union should not be able to donate to a candidate that is not the endorsed candidate of that party.

CA Why do you take that view that a political party shouldn't donate to a candidate who is not endorsed?

W Transparency.

CA Assuming, though, that such a donation was properly disclosed, is the transparency not achieved by the disclosure method?

W. When you understand the significance that electors place on independents, or independence of their councillors, we believe that's a necessary step.

(South-east Queensland 'independent' council elections are dominated by candidates who are either members of or close supporters of political parties. Not all unions are affiliated with the Labor Party. Under Mr Hallam's plan, are unaffiliated unions allowed to support 'independent' candidates? And are affiliated unionists and party members to be prevented from 'in-kind' support such as being polling booth workers? In my opinion, Mr Hallam's proposal of banning party and union donations to 'independents' is undesirable and unworkable.)

W The last time a major political party tried to involve itself in an election outside of Brisbane City was the Gold Coast in 2008. That party spent $1 million. They ran in every seat, every division and the mayoralty and didn't succeed. People are happy for you to be a member of a party, they'll live with that, but they expect you to be fiercely independent when you walk into the council chamber.

CA Related to that, as you know, most candidates for local government are not party endorsed?

W Correct.

CA And a good many campaign on the basis of independence?

W True.

CA As if that is an electoral virtue?

W Correct. I think I've said that, yes.

CA You, by the sound of it, would favour some greater listing of the attributes of a group?
W Yes.
CA Whereas at present a group is one which is formed to promote the election of candidates or to share in the benefits of fundraising?
W Correct. I think we all struggle with the complexities of the electoral law and, indeed, what happens once you get elected. The fundamental difference between local government and state and federal governments is that we don't have a party political system. I think that's a good thing. But we're talking about mums and dads. We're talking about, as you have heard in evidence, people that don't have access to parties. They don't have access to party-sanctioned lawyers. They don't have Crown Law advice. They don't have a whole lot of things.

(Though he likes fiercely independent councillors, Mr Hallam is putting some cogent points as to why parties or some such groups of councillors would be more accountable at local government level.)

CA Some don't look at the Act.
W Well, that has come out in evidence, yes. I should just say this, though: we are the level of government closest to the people. We are most reflective of community. A lot of folks do not have a background in understanding the separation of powers, the operations of government, the executive, the judiciary or even the most rudimentary ideas about how governments work. They are motivated because they want to serve their community and/or they have

some particular issue that they want to address. So in that sense, we're most reflective of society, I guess, and the corollary of that is that we're probably in some ways least prepared.

(Do we really want council candidates who don't have 'even the most rudimentary ideas about how governments work'? We do have some quite intelligent mums and dads who can do basic research, and have comprehension skills.)

CA One issue that has been considered in this hearing is the use of trusts and other forms of intermediary between donors and candidate recipients. Does the association support the notion of donations to a trust, which would then distribute funds to one or more beneficiary candidates?

W We don't have a position but we do support the notion of a separate bank account.

CA Do you think candidates should know who the donors are to a trust from which they're receiving money?

W It depends on what the question is. It's different from owning shares in a company or having some financial connection and the potential for gain or loss by way of a decision. That doesn't exist in the case of a political donation. It's not the same thing. If you by extension start to think about banning donations and the like, or banning donations from classes of people, you completely change the nature of the process.

(A Progressive would insist reflective change is often a good thing.)

CA Well, you ventured into the area of conflict of interests and mentioned, I think, material personal interests as one aspect of that?
W Correct, yes.
CA The other aspect is a conflict of interest?
W Correct.
CA What's the difference between the two?
W A material interest, as I said earlier, is where the Act is quite clear there is potential for financial gain or loss by a decision council might take, that you have a direct financial or pecuniary interest. We tell everyone that if you have an MPI, as soon as you register, you walk; you do not stay. That is just black-and-white advice we give all day, every day.

(The dichotomy is often understood as actual conflict of interest and perceived conflict of interest.)
CA You leave open, by the sound of it, to the individual the question of whether they walk where there is a conflict of interest?
W Correct. We advise them on what the law says and then tell them it's up to them as to how they deal with their conflict.
CA Dealing with conflict of interests, that would leave to the decision of the individual as to whether, having declared a conflict, he or she remains to vote on a proposal or not?
W That's correct, yes.
CA Does that, in turn, place reliance on the integrity of that councillor?
W It's not a question of integrity. I mean, they're either being lawful or not lawful. It's a matter for

them and their conscience and, I guess, the broader electorate in terms of whether you get elected at the next term or not.

(Counsel Assisting, Mr Rice, is correct, IMO. There are shades of grey between lawful and unlawful as the Act requires the subjective call of a councillor. The CCC in its Operation Belcarra recommendations wants the call on conflicts of interest transferred to the other councillors.)

CA And is the ultimate sanction, then, the next election?

W Correct. I mean, as an old veteran of 30-odd years in local government, we go through these swings where we are either pro-development or anti-development, and there is a cycle and you see it. Probably the cycle comes around more often now than it did years ago.

CA Before we started talking about these conflicts and the resolution of them, we were talking about the use of trusts. Does the use of a trust as an intermediary between a donor and the recipient enable a candidate to genuinely avoid making a declaration of interest?

W I've never really contemplated it, to be honest.

CA I ask that because if the disclosure regime is working, then the third party, being the trust, should make its own disclosure of who its donors are.

W True. That was the intention, that they had a complete system, it was indivisible, that there was a check and balance in relation to one of three parties having to report that – the donor, the recipient and the trustee - so that there was a complete picture of any transactions that occurred.

CA And all these returns are made public by the Electoral Commission; correct?

W Correct.

CA On their website?

W That's right.

CA So that the information is published to the world?

W Correct.

CA As to, for example, who the donors are to a recipient trust?

W That's right.

CA And then, from there, where the trust distributes its money to?

W Correct.

CA In that scenario, then, would it be disingenuous to any degree for a candidate to decry knowledge of who the donors to a trust are when it's available to the public at large?

W I have never turned my mind to that possibility.

CA Do you subscribe to the view that the deliberation process, including the recording of minutes and so forth, will sufficiently expose conflicts and the way they're treated?

W Yes, and, as I said earlier, all the reports are made available. They're public documents, those planning reports. All of the debate and the actual decision, the actual resolution, the passing, must be done in full open council. And the final check is, as I said earlier, by law, where the council overturns the recommendation of the planner, it must state in its reasons why that is the case. So I think that ties it up beautifully.

(If you look at the minutes of council meetings you will notice very little debate. Debate has been held elsewhere, often in places the public is excluded from.)

CA On the subject of donations, you are not in favour of any other kind of banning of donations beyond the one that you have mentioned?

W No. No, we have turned our mind to it, and I guess it will be for the High Court one day, but there are clearly these concepts of the implied right of political freedom of speech and association.

CA What about capping of campaign donations up to a particular limit?

W My association doesn't have a view. A personal view is I think that has some merit.

CA What about public funding?. Would you favour some component of public funding?

W No, because we're putting our hand in the ratepayers' pocket.

CA What about expenditure caps?

W Well, I think that would probably go – it's a difficult one because do you penalise the individual who is able to fund their own campaign versus someone who is externally funded? Yes, I haven't got a resolved view on that. So I guess what's the definition of good public policy? One that you can enforce and one that improves the system.

8

I HAVE TAKEN AN INTEREST in Queensland corruption, its causes and discontents, since the Fitzgerald Inquiry into police corruption of 1987-89. By understanding the origins and growth of corruption, we can better discover effective remedies, the law of unintended consequences notwithstanding.

I offer what I see are common conditions for corruption in the police force and politics. I have arranged them in what I consider might be the force of their influence:

- The feeling among the corrupt their work deserves more remuneration than is provided. It could be a police officer who thinks they are putting their life on the line at work or a politician who thinks that long working hours away from family are dismissed by the public. One councillor would regularly tell me about the long hours of his job. These feelings of deserving more and being under-appreciated can be accompanied by resentment and exacerbated by stress.
- Time. It takes time to build a network of effective corruption. This is another reason for capping the length of service of councillors and mayors.

- An estimation that the chances of getting caught or being severely dealt with are slim. This estimation is a good calculation. Illegal bookmakers, pimps, and brothel-keepers were paying off Queensland police for decades before the practice was exposed in the late 1980s.

In my novel, *Iraqi Icicle*, I have a fictional retelling of how Queensland Police Commissioner (1958-1969) Franck Bischoff was paid off by illegal SP bookies who also traded legally at Brisbane racetracks. Every Saturday, after the last race, one bookmaker would write in his ledger a winning bet for Mr Bischoff.

I will always remember the surreal and blackly humorous moment in the 1970s when friends and I gathered around a TV in an illegal casino in the Valley to watch the 6 o'clock news. There on the television was Minister Russ Hinze telling us there were no illegal casinos in Fortitude Valley.

Today, corrupt politicians rarely get caught and one does jail time every blue moon. No wonder astute retired judges are calling for a federal anti-corruption commission.

- Justifications such as it does not harm anyone or I need to do it to continue my good work. Corruption does enormous harm from taking money from the public purse, to encouraging similar bad behaviour or cynicism and despair among those who learn of it, and

detracting from the lifestyles of citizens through bad planning and policy decisions.
- Thinking of it as a sport. There are some people out there who enjoy gaming the system, and using dupes in council and the media to put one over other people. They have the mindset of an adolescent sticking a sign on a classmate while pretending to be patting them on the back.
- Disdain for the public. Corrupt officials lose sight of their roles as servants of the public. They assume the roles of beloved masters. Father knows best.

From the professionalisation of councils in the 1990s to hefty pay rises on amalgamations, councillors have attained remuneration well in excess of the community median and what they were paid in previous jobs.

From memory, I provide a run-down of some of the previous jobs of councillors from one Pine Rivers Shire council: postman, graphic artist, teacher, an accountant, a businessman whose business was rumoured to be in bad financial shape, picture framer, public servant, bank manager, lawyer, and soldier. The myth that politicians could earn more money on the outside is not true of most councillors.

For the record, during the 2015/16 financial year, Moreton Bay Mayor Allan Sutherland received a salary of $210,396, plus an employer superannuation contribution of $25,248.

Councillors who served the full financial year received $127,740 and super of $15,329.

A smartphone, tablet, notepad and other computer equipment were provided to each councillor at an average cost of $2075 a year. Councillors were provided with a fully maintained vehicle at an average cost of $13,636 a year. In accordance with policy, councillors make a contribution to offset their private usage of these vehicles. Division 6 Councillor Koliana Winchester opted to use her own private motor vehicle and not be provided with a fully maintained vehicle from council.

We should not begrudge full-time councillors adequate salaries if we choose to structure our local governments that way but you would hope that mixing with wealthy developers would not inspire unnecessary greed.

9

The ELECTORAL COMMISSION of Queesland administers various matters relating to state and local Governernment elections. One such matter is reviewing political donations. 'I need to ensure that the people of Queensland have confidence in the electoral events that are being conducted which impact on them,' ECQ commissioner Walter van der Merwe told the CCC hearing.

How's that coming along, Counsel Assisting, Greg Rice, asked the commissioner.

'There were allegations which were made to me,' Mr Van der Merwe said. 'I operate on the basis that I'd rather hear about it than not hear about it, and some of those allegations, I thought, were reasonably significant, but they needed further investigation and review and I think that's why we are here (at the CCC Fortitude Valley HQ) today.'

Indeed the commissioner had sent to the CCC concerns about Moreton Futures Trust and other issues relating to the 2016 Moreton Bay Regional Council elections. I know this because I asked. I do not know whether the ECQ passed on similar information about the Gold Coast and Ipswich City elections. There was some speculation the Ipswich and Gold Coast inquiries were already in motion and

Moreton Bay was added after the ECQ request for investigation.

I am pretty sure my inquires of the ECQ concerning Moreton Futures Trust in part prompted the CCC referral. I pointed out the 2012 trust third-party declaration did not have the name nor address of trustee John Ryan.

CA The next option, in paragraph (b), relates to gifts made out of a trust fund, where the relevant information comprises the names and residential or business addresses of the trustees or any other person responsible for the funds of the foundation?

W (Mr van der Merwe) Yes.

CA It might assist you to go to section 130 at page 106. It provides for a person to make a query about the content of disclosure returns? A query could take the form of a complaint, I suppose?

W It could.

CA Does that happen?

W It does. I am obliged, then, to investigate it. I can't turn a blind eye to it because there could be some element of truth in the allegations. So it needs to be looked at, and we do.

Counsel Assisting, Mr Rice, asked if there were any prosecutions for incomplete or incorrect disclosure regarding the 2016 council elections.

Mr van der Merwe said the answer was no.

Were there any from the 2012 council elections?

The answer was no.

'I don't have the capacity to make sure that they follow the legislation,' Mr van der Merwe told the inquiry.

Still, the system is working. 'It's transparent. It's actually working,' Mr van der Merwe said. They (the voters) know where the money is coming from. They know where the money is being spent. If for whatever reason a candidate chooses not to do that, one would hope they would eventually get caught out.'

It seems a trifle strange for the Electoral Commissioner to be sitting at an inquiry into the elections of four of Queensland's biggest councils and saying the system is working.

For a start, an authority, such as the Department of Local Government, the Electoral Commission, or local councils, needs to take responsibility for translating the relevant acts from the language of lawyers to plain English. About six or so years ago, I found that government media sections started referring me to a website or an act of parliament rather than answering my questions. Now it is nice to be able to refer to such primary sources but media departments are there to explain what can be complex documentation in terms the average media consumer would understand. But the thought processes of the media section and its workers seemed to be, 'Am I liable or is my department liable if I say the wrong thing or I am misinterpreted.'

I am sorry, but that excuse does not cut it. One of roles of a media officer and other public servants is to be a translator. I only studied law for six months and I mean studied in the loosest possible sense. So I take it there is a valid reason why laws are written in script often impenetrable of the average mind. Here is the first mention of disclosure periods in the Local Government Electoral Act 2011:

Part 6 Electoral funding and financial disclosure
Division 1 Preliminary
106 Definitions for part
In this part—
candidate's disclosure period means the disclosure period applying to the candidate under division 2, subdivision 1.
disclosure date, for a return, means the day prescribed by regulation for the return.

As LGAQ CEO Greg Hallam said, political parties have access to experts who can translate such complex laws for all their candidates. But independents are left to their own devices and are at the mercy of a public service dreading making a mistake for which they might be held culpable.

I support compulsory information meetings for aspiring candidates as well as a one-stop website where the relevant legislation is explained in as simple terms as possible without the need for complementary explanations elsewhere. I want to know what the disclosure period means not that I should refer to division 2, subdivision 1 to find out.

I would favour a candidate hotline for questions about donations and disclosure. Finally with all these mechanisms in place, I would like the Electoral Commission to have an enforcement program which includes naming and shaming on the ECQ website.

The Electoral Commission has a new system EDS for providing real-time (obligations within seven business days) disclosure of political gifts. Data in reports available to the public are as uploaded by donors and candidates. But here's the rub: The ECQ does not verify or validate this data. Without enforcement, the dishonest, not declaring donations from vested interests, or gaming the system in other ways, have the advantage over the honest. As 19th century jurist Charles Bowen pointed out, it rains equally on the just and the unjust but the unjust has stolen the umbrella from the just.

Transcript #5
Abridged by Bernie Dowling

Witness Walter van der Merwe, April 18, 2017
PO, Presiding Officer Alan MacSporran QC
CA, Counsel Assisting, Glen Rice QC
W, Witness Walter van der Merwe

CA Sir, is your name Walter van der Merwe?
W It is.
CA Are you the Electoral Commissioner of Queensland?
W I am.

CA   Could you explain your role as Electoral Commissioner in relation to local government elections carried out in 2016?

W   Basically the Electoral Commission of Queensland ran the 2016 quadrennial elections for local governments, as I did in 2012, that is, from the beginning to the end, from the announcement of the electoral events through to assisting candidates in terms of their nominations and the polling day, which happened in March, and the confirmation of the candidates who were elected.

CA You have Commission staff to assist you in that function?

W I do, yes.

CA How many full-time staff are in the Commission?

W As of today, I have 43 FTEs.

(FTE stands for full-time equivalents. Some bureaucrats seem to think acronyms are self-explanatory. IDKW.)

CA You mentioned, I think, when you were speaking a moment ago, about an electoral event or an election event?

W Yes.

CA What do you mean by that term?

W   If we run, say, for example, local government quadrennial elections, we term that as an event. We employ close to 10,000 temporary staff to assist with that. We also employ a number of returning officers, who are responsible for each local government area. So it's not all run by my permanent full-time equivalents in Mary Street.

CA How many council elections were there in 2016?
W In 2016, we had 1787 candidate nominations for the council elections – more than ever before. There were 77 mayoral ballots, 218 councillor ballots for divided council areas and 284 council elections for 54 undivided council ballots.
CA How does an event of that size compare, say, with a state government election?
W The state government election, we focus on 89 electoral districts. A local government election is, as you can see by the numbers, a lot more complex and challenging.
CA Tell me, did the Electoral Commission receive complaints subsequent to the 2016 elections concerning practices and conduct of candidates?
W I did.
CA What level of complaint compared, say, to the preceding election?
W Compared to the 2012, I believe the level of complaints was significantly higher.
CA Is there any reason you could discern from the nature and content of those complaints?
W Not really. A number of those complaints weren't necessarily against all council areas. They were focused predominantly down the coast and in Ipswich, so Moreton Bay, Ipswich and the Gold Coast.
CA I want to discuss with you some of the structure of the Local Government Electoral Act and some of the requirements that are imposed on candidates. First of all, you would be aware, would you not, Mr

van der Merwe that section 3 of the Act identifies that the purpose of it is to ensure transparent conduct of elections with respect to local government elections?
W I'm aware of that.
CA Is that in fact something that guides you in the performance of your function?
W Oh, it is. I need to ensure that the people of Queensland have confidence in the electoral events that are being conducted which impact on them.
CA Would it be right to say that with the exception of the Brisbane City Council, most candidates are not endorsed by political parties?
W That is correct. Candidates in local governments are basically individual candidates.
CA There is provision, is there not, for the Commission to receive a record of membership of a group of candidates?
W If candidates wish to run as a group, they need to advise the Commission. There was one group in Moreton (Your Community First), I believe, that ran as a group. There were candidates up north as well that ran as a group.
CA The expression "group of candidates", I think, has a particular definition, being a group formed either to promote the election of candidates or to share in the benefits of fundraising to promote the election of the candidates?
W Yes, that's as it's described in the legislation.
CA (Regarding donations) There are a number of options provided for, I think you will see in section 109: firstly, where the gift (donation) is made by

members of an unincorporated association, and the kind of information that is required involves not only the name of the association but the names and residential or business addresses of members of the executive?

W That's correct, yes.

CA Would you expect, in the ordinary course, that that would be a post office box or a street address?

W I would expect it to be a street address.

CA Could you tell us when such a return is required to be lodged?

W Candidates and groups of candidates in an election must provide a disclosure return to the Commission within 15 weeks after polling day.

CA Can I ask you this: does that regime of submission of a disclosure return up to 15 weeks after polling day assist an elector to know who has funded a candidate's campaign before they lodge a vote?

W Possibly not.

CA Is it correct to say that the nub of it is that the candidate receiving the gifts should know the names of persons behind gifts of $200 or more?

W They should.

CA That is perhaps not necessarily the donors; it could be the trustees of the trust that receives money from donors?

W That is absolutely correct.

(Candidates should be obliged to know who the donors to a trust are, IMO. It becomes complicated in the case of a union donation because you are not going to name every union member. But you pay lawyers the big bucks to resolve such anomalies.)

CA But the candidate should know the names of the person from whom the money is being received?

W They should, that's right.

CA And should not receive a gift otherwise?

W They should not receive it if they don't know where it is coming from.

CA Where it is coming from includes the name of the person providing it?

W That's correct.

CA And not only the name, the residential or business address of that person?

W That's right, the particulars.

CA Likewise, however, with respect to loans received, the details of the loan have to be declared in the disclosure return?

W They do.

PO Mr Rice, just excuse me one moment. Mr van der Merwe you said real-time disclosure wouldn't work. Is that a logistical technology issue, or why do you say it won't work, real-time disclosure?

W Because when a gift is made, it is done all electronically. It goes on to the system. By way of example, if I give candidate A, X amount of money, I can put that on as a gift. Candidate A actually needs to receive that. So the parliament decided on let's wait seven days and then it will be published. But it is a lot better than publishing it after the event.

(And worse than banning donations from seven business days before an election. If people infringe, 'and they shall know that I am the ECQ when I shall lay my vengeance upon them'. Thanks, Samuel L. Jackson.)

PO I suppose it is still open to – "abuse" might not be the right word, but circumvention of the intent of it, transparency wise, by people donating within the seven days prior to the polling day so that that donation will not be disclosed?

W You are correct.

(Mr MacSporran was spot on. That is exactly what happened at the first test of the new disclosure laws at the Ipswich mayoral by-election. The lawyers framing such laws just have to get them completely right.)

PO One way around it, I suppose, would be to prohibit the receipt of donations within that seven-day period?

W Within seven days of polling day.

PO In that way, everything that was donated would be in fact disclosed prior to the polling day?

W That's correct, but if I was given a system to operate – I purely administer the system, but that has got to be a policy decision by the government.

PO I understand.

W But certainly if that was a recommendation and it was adopted, it would be very easy to implement.

(The Operation Belcarra report recommended ceasing donations seven business days before election day. Candidates must return any gifts received after that date. Of course, the CCC is making recommendations and not giving binding instructions to State Parliament.)

PO Thank you. Thank you, Mr Rice.

CA If you have a query or a complaint concerning the content of a disclosure return, what is the means by which you investigate that further?

W We will have a discussion with the individual, the candidate or whoever put the return in and ascertain is it correct. We will also allow them to put in an amended return if they realise they have made a mistake. So, yes, they are afforded the opportunity to explain the full content of their return, and I would certainly accept an amended return as long as it was accurate and truthful.

CA The Act requires you to keep a register of these returns; correct?

W Yes, we keep a register of all returns.

CA By that means, the public can scrutinise –

W They can.

(The ECQ has records dating from the council elections of 2012, as the electoral act approving the system was passed in 2011.)

CA The records are available for physical inspection also?

W You can make an appointment, and we will provide you with a hard copy to inspect.

CA Obviously it's more convenient these days to just go to a computer?

W To do it over the net, yes.

CA Anyone who wants to do that, go to a computer, can look it up on your website?

W They can.

CA So far as the completeness or accuracy of returns is concerned, leaving aside the query or complaint scenario, is there any means that the Commission has or employs to verify returns?

W We do random sampling for local government where we will do an audit of the return. Due to the sheer quantum, we don't audit every single one.

CA Does the Commission have the means to go about a comparison and reconciliation of candidate returns as opposed to what is disclosed on third party returns – to see whether they match, in other words?

W There is a capacity to do it. We don't do it all the time. As I say, we do sample reconciliations and reviews of returns in local government.

CA How, though, do you ascertain whether all donations are in fact listed?

W It would be very difficult to ascertain that.

CA Is that reliant on the honesty of the candidate?

W I have to take it on good faith of the candidate and the person submitting the return.

CA You don't have enforcement staff as such, I think you have said?

W I don't.

CA For the 2016 election, which is now over a year ago, were any offences identified, that is to say, has anyone been prosecuted for incomplete or incorrect disclosure on their disclosure returns?

W As far as prosecuted, no.

CA Were there any from the 2012 election, do you know?

W I don't believe so.

CA There was something else that you have touched on, but I haven't really asked you anything about it. There is an additional requirement, is there not, for a candidate to operate, for the purpose of a campaign, a dedicated bank account?

W That is correct. Candidates and groups of candidates must keep a separate account with the financial institution for the running of their election campaigns. The account is known as a dedicated account.

CA Does the Commission have the means to try to vet or scrutinise whether a candidate is using such an account, at least for the operation of law, it being an offence not to do so?

W There is an assumption that a candidate will have an operating account. And the details of that account, the ingoings and outgoings, you know, we can certainly have a look at that.

We can't cover for a candidate who might run two or three accounts. As far as we are concerned, the legislation says you have one and that's what you run with. If you have two or three and you are caught out, you then commit an offence and you will be prosecuted for that.

(Ipswich Councillor Paul Tully was caught out with two accounts. Would he be prosecuted? As it turned out, no.

The CCC handed down its loftily titled report, *Operation Belcarra – A blueprint for integrity and addressing corruption risk in local government* to State Parliament on October 4, 2017.

It read in part, 'The CCC formed the view that Cr Tully failed to operate a dedicated bank account in compliance with section 126 of the LGE Act and determined there was sufficient evidence to refer this matter to the ECQ for consideration of any prosecution proceedings it considers warranted. However, given the systemic nature of this issue, the CCC determined to take no further action. In any event, a prosecution for an offence against section 126 of the LGE Act must be commenced within 12 months from when the offence occurred (20 April 2016.)'

The CCC rendered an opinion on whether they would have recommended a prosecution had such a course not been invalidated for being out of time. The CCC would not have recommended prosecution. Yet, Cr Tully and others found to be operating more than one account admitted they knew of their obligations regarding a dedicated account. In this context the word 'systemic' used by the CCC as a reason for non-prosecution would seem to mean 'they are all doing it,' which, as I have suggested elsewhere, is a troublesome excuse for ignoring illegality.)

CA   That is Mr van der Merwe's evidence, Mr Chairman.

10

PEOPLE LIKE TO GIVE Moreton Bay Regional Council Deputy Mayor Mike Charlton money, come election time.

Before the amalgamation of Pine Rivers and Caboolture Shires in 2008, an organisation called Friends of Pine Rivers gave Councillor Charlton $15,000 to fight the 2004 Pine Rivers Shire Council election. It was a windfall for Cr Charlton as the money could have gone elsewhere. Five councillors, including Mayor Yvonne Chapman and Deputy Mayor Bryan Galvin, were elected unopposed so they did not need campaign funds.

The 2004 election saw bad blood rise between Pine Rivers Shire councillors and me when I wrote in the Pine Rivers Press it was a shame to see four electoral divisions and the mayoralty ending in no-contest. The five Councillors involved, and some others who were not, vehemently told me it was a sign the public considered they were doing a great job. It was churlish of me to see it in any other light.

At the inaugural Moreton Bay Regional Council 2008 election, a mob called Advancing Moreton Leadership gave Councillor Charlton $20,000. It took me a while to find out what Advancing Moreton Leadership was but I got my man, Greg

Bowden, CEO of Advancing Brisbane Leadership. This trust, associated with the conservative political party, the Liberal Party, had raised $2.3 million to re-elect then Brisbane Lord Mayor Campbell Newman and his fellow Liberal candidates. So successful was Mr Bowden at fundraising that the organisation had more money than needed to fight Brisbane council elections.

When he finally returned my phone calls, Mr Bowden said it was within the remit of Advancing Brisbane Leadership to support conservative candidates in the Moreton Bay Region just north of Brisbane to keep the Red Menace of the Labor Party from engaging in border skirmishes and building influence in Brisbane. Mr Bowden said something like that to me.

On a cheery Wednesday afternoon Mike Charlton appeared as a witness before the Operation Belcarra Crime and Corruption Commission (CCC) hearing into the 2016 council elections of Moreton Bay, the Gold Coast and Ipswich.

It was the second day of the inquiry at which Alan MacSporran was presiding officer and Glen Rice was Counsel Assisting.

Mr Rice asked Cr Charlton questions about his co-operation with mayoral candidate Allan Sutherland at the 2016 election.

This included Cr Charlton letterboxing an endorsement letter from Cr Sutherland with a joint how-to-vote card on the back.

'My thought process was simply I think there's some benefit potentially in that, so I accepted the offer,' Cr Charlton said.

He ran for Division 9 as an independent in 2012 and 2016 after running successfully in 2008 as a member of a group with unsuccessful mayoral candidate Bryan Galvin.

Counsel Assisting, Mr Rice, told the hearing, 'Under the 2011 Act, a group has to be registered with the Electoral Commission giving notice of who the members of the group are and other details.'

Cr Charlton said, 'The way I view the word "independent" is that I'm not obligated to anybody else, that I am free to make the decisions that I see fit, and certainly when it comes to holding office, there is no obligation upon me to vote any particular way to honour a commitment to anyone else.'

He said he had intended to split the cost of producing the endorsement letter but it did not work out that way.

'My intent, the decision to do the letter, was for me to pay 50 per cent,' Cr Charlton said. 'Post-election, Allan offered to pay for the whole lot, and my response was I would accept that, but it had to be declared as a third party declaration, which it was.'

Cr Charlton and Cr Sutherland had a joint how-to-vote card with the slogan 'For a bright future'.

'Again, Allan offered to pay for the entire cost, which, again, was part of that declaration,' Cr Charlton said.

Cr Sutherland, Cr Charlton, and Cr Mick Gillam appeared together on a campaign billboard off Gympie Rd, in the area known locally as the Bald Hills Flats.

The invoice for that billboard was made out to 'A Bright Future for Moreton'.

'I was going to pay a percentage of the billboard and when it came time for that to be arranged, the Mayor again offered to pick up my share as well as his share and, again, my response was I would accept that, but it had to be part of that third party declaration, which it was then, and is,' Cr Charlton told the hearing.

Incumbent councillors must fill out an interests register every 30 days but Cr Sutherland made the offers to Cr Charlton after the election and they were not recorded on Cr Charlton's interests register before the election.

Mr Rice spoke about another billboard on Anzac Avenue which had the images of Cr Sutherland, Division 6 candidate Koliana Winchester, and Division 5 candidate James Houghton.

Cr Charlton said he had made preliminary inquiries to the provider of that billboard 'simply as assistance to the Mayor'.

Cr Charlton was asked about his fundraising efforts at the 2016 election and his requirement to keep a dedicated bank record of the financial aspects of his campaign.

He said Bryan Galvin organised a fundraiser in March 2016 at the Excelsior Football Club at Albany

Creek which raised thousands of dollars for his campaign. 'It was in the middle of the election campaign, so I had no role in that at all,' Cr Charlton told the hearing.

Cr Charlton was also asked about his association with the trustees of Moreton Futures Trust, a substantial donor to Cr Sutherland in 2012 and 2016. 'I've known (Trustee) Kirby (Leeke) for a long time, through family associations and associations with the Masonic Lodge,' Cr Charlton said.

'Dr John (Ryan) has been my personal physician for quite some years now,' Cr Charlton said.

'I was part of the discussions and the concept for the formation of the trust, and then there was a change in legislation, there was a change in trustees, and I determined to not have any active role in the trust from, off the top of my head, early 2012, prior to the 2012 election,' Cr Charlton said.

He said he was aware of some trust fundraising activities. 'I'm aware of an event out at Lakeside, a motorsport day. In fact, I think there was more than one, I think there was two. I think there was a corporate dinner.'

Transcript #6
Abridged by Bernie Dowling

Witness Councillor Mike Charlton, April 19, 2017
PO, Presiding Officer Alan MacSporran QC
CA, Counsel Assisting, Glen Rice QC
W, Witness Councillor Mike Charlton

CA Is your name Michael Keith Charlton?
W Yes, it is.
CA Mr Charlton, you are Deputy Mayor of Moreton Bay Regional Council?
W Yes.
CA Could I start with a little bit of background, Mr Charlton. You first became a councillor, I think, in 1994?
W Yes.
CA Would that have been to Pine Rivers at that stage?
W It was.
CA And you've successfully contested every local government election since?
W That's correct.
CA The amalgamation occurred in 2008?
W Yes.
CA And so you've been the councillor for Division 9 since 2008?
W Correct.
CA I'll just ask you, firstly, about the 2008 election. One feature of it, I think, was that you and another gentleman, called Brian Battersby, campaigned as a group; is that correct?
W Bryan Galvin.
CA Bryan Galvin, was it? Sorry.
W Bryan Galvin was the mayoral candidate.

(Solicitor Bryan Galvin's name kept cropping up at the hearing without any sinister overtimes. It was just co-incidental. Yet it reminded me of a line from

the classic film, *The Third Man*: 'There was a third man. He didn't give evidence.')
CA Did you join with him for campaign purposes?
W Yes, I did.
CA As a group?
W Correct.
CA Was there a scheme of declaration or registration of a group at that stage?
W I'm not sure what a scheme of declaration is.
CA Well, you know under the 2011 Act, a group has to be registered with the Electoral Commission giving notice of who the members of the group are and other details; did you know that?
W Under the 2011 Act?
CA 2011, yes.
W But we're talking about the 2008 election, aren't we?
CA We are, yes. Was there such a scheme in 2008?
W I don't recall. I recall registering as a group, but I don't recall a scheme.
CA What was the purpose of joining with him as a group for the purpose of that election?
W I supported Bryan as the mayoral candidate. It was for convenience of operation in manning polling booths and for funding of campaign.
CA What advantages did it have for campaign purposes?
W Well, there were two campaigns. Where there was commonality in approach to the campaign around manning of booths in my division, I supplied workers

to – in fact, I think I had a joint How to Vote Card with Bryan in 2008.

CA There was some resource sharing?

W There was.

CA Anything more than that?

W Well, there was the financial – my campaign was financed through the group.

CA Did you do joint fundraising then?

W I attended some fundraisers with Brian, yes, I did.

CA When you contested the 2012 election, did you do so as an independent or as a member of a group?

W As an independent.

CA And likewise in 2016?

W Yes.

CA As an independent?

W As an independent.

CA Can I just ask you for your view on what is the content of the expression "independent" as it applies to you?

W Well, that's a good question. I guess the way I view the word "independent" is that I'm not obligated to anybody else, that I am free to make the decisions that I see fit, and certainly when it comes to holding office, there is no obligation upon me to vote any particular way to honour a commitment to anyone else.

CA For the 2016 elections, did you promote yourself using the word "independent"?

W I don't recall. Look, I may have, but I'm –

CA Some people make quite a thing of it and others don't want to do so. I'm just wondering where you fit in the scheme of things.
W I certainly view myself as an independent character.
CA In your interface with electors, though, is that something you promote to them?
W Correct.

(In 2008, Cr Charlton received $20,000 from Advancing Moreton Leadership, associated with the Liberal Party.)

CA You know, of course, the Mayor, Allan Sutherland?
W I do.
CA You didn't pay him (in 2016), though, for the fact of his writing you a letter of endorsement?
W No, I did not. No.
CA Okay. You have used joint How to Vote Cards in the past, haven't you?
W I've used joint How to Vote Cards for some time, I think off the top of my head back to 1997, but I don't have records that go back that far, so I'm not 100 per cent sure.
CA You did so in 2016?
W Yes.
CA There was a joint How to Vote Card with Mr Sutherland?
W Correct.
CA You would appear jointly to have adopted the slogan "For a bright future"; correct?
W Correct.

CA Do you know what the origin was of that set of words, "For a bright future", that appear on that How to Vote Card?

W The first I heard that slogan was at the launch of the university site concept. I thought it was a good slogan and put the "Bright ideas for a bright future" on the front of it.

CA Which university site, Mr Charlton?

W That's the Petrie University site, now known as The Mill PDA.

CA Was there cost sharing associated with the use of that How to Vote Card?

W Again, there was to be cost sharing. That was my intent at the time of the production of the How to Vote Cards. And, again, Allan offered to pay for the entire cost, which, again, was part of that declaration.

CA Would you accept that a person looking at that How to Vote Card would think that you and Mr Sutherland were mutually supporting each other for election purposes?

W You could deduce that, yes.

CA Having had an arrangement with him for the use of a joint How to Vote Card, did you pause at any time to consider whether that might give rise to at least a perception that you and he were a group of candidates?

W No. No, I did not. I would say that that How to Vote Card, by your own statement, clearly shows that I was supporting the Mayor as the mayoral candidate, but not as a group.

(The Operation Belcarra report found Cr Charlton was among councillors who misunderstood what constituted a group.

'The CCC's view, however, is that voters are entitled to have as clear and unambiguous understanding as possible of the financial and political relationships between candidates. In the CCC's view, candidates and councillors' failure to recognise how these practices could give rise to perceptions that they were campaigning as a group may, at least in part, reflect their poor understanding of what a group is. Some believed that a group required candidates to have common policies and shared values, but this is not reflected in the LGE Act definition.'

The Operation Belcarra report recommended a group be defined by what they did and not by what they said they believed in.

'A group of candidates is defined by the behaviours of the group and/or its members rather than the purposes for which the group was formed.

'For example: A group of candidates means a group of individuals, each of whom is a candidate for the election, where the candidates:

- receive the majority of their campaign funding from a common or shared source; or
- have a common or shared campaign strategy (e.g. shared policies, common slogans and branding); or
- use common or shared campaign resources (e.g. campaign workers, signs); or

- engage in cooperative campaigning activities, including using shared how-to-vote cards, engaging in joint advertising (e.g. on billboards) or formally endorsing another candidate.')

CA   There were other shared promotional arrangements, weren't there?

W There were.

CA There was a billboard; correct?

W Yes.

CA You shared a billboard with Mayor Sutherland and Councillor Gillam?

W Correct.

CA That was positioned, was it, on Gympie Road towards Bald Hills Flats?

W Correct.

CA Was there a payment sharing arrangement between the three of you for the use of that joint billboard?

W Again, there was to be – I was going to pay a percentage of the billboard and when it came time for that to be arranged, the Mayor again offered to pick up my share as well as his share and, again, my response was I would accept that, but it had to be part of that third party declaration, which it was then, and is.

CA Can I change the subject a bit and ask you about whether you're aware of an entity called the Moreton Futures Trust?

W Yes, I am.

CA Do you know Kirby Leeke and Dr John Ryan?

W Yes, I do.
CA Just take them in turn. First of all Kirby Leeke, how do you know him?
W I've known Kirby for a long time, through family associations and associations with the Masonic Lodge.
CA Going back how far, can you estimate?
W Oh, probably close to 35 to 40 years.
CA And Dr John Ryan, how do you know him?
W Dr John has been my personal physician for quite some years now and he was practising in Albany Creek where I have lived since 1980, and he was also a mutual friend of Bryan Galvin's.
CA What do you know about the origin of Moreton Futures Trust?
W Moreton Futures Trust was set up as a vehicle to raise funds to fund election campaigns for candidates, as determined by the trustee, as I understand it.
CA About how long ago, can you estimate?
W Oh, look, I'm not 100 per cent sure, but sometime between 2008 and 2012.
CA Do you know of any connection between Kirby Leeke and Dr John Ryan and the Moreton Futures Trust?
W In that they're trustees.
CA Well, are they trustees to your knowledge?
W My understanding is that they are trustees, yes.
CA Do you know what is the purpose of the trust's existence?

CA Do you know how persons associated with the trust raised money?

W I'm aware of some fundraising activities, but not necessarily all.

CA What kind? What kind of activities are you aware of?

W I'm aware of an event out at Lakeside, a motor sport day. In fact, I think there was more than one, I think there was two. I think there was a corporate dinner.

CA Do you know whether Mayor Sutherland received funds from Moreton Futures Trust for the 2016 campaign?

W I believe he did.

CA Was it ever a subject of discussion between you and him going into the 2016 election?

W In what way?

CA Well, as to how he might be funded and whether there might be some benefits to him from that?

W He may have made statements that he was being funded by the trust, but it wasn't a topic of discussion, or an involvement that I had.

CA Were you ever offered money from the Moreton Futures Trust?

W In the 2016 election?

CA Yes.

W No.

CA Had you been offered money prior to that?

W Yes.

CA In which election?

W 2012.

CA Did you receive money on that occasion?
W I did, which is on my declaration, a $5,000 loan which was repaid in full.
CA Can I show you this disclosure return, Mr Charlton. Just confirm for us that that's your disclosure return dated 1 July 2016?
W Yes, I believe so.
CA If you look at page 2, it describes the amount of gifts received as being just under $14,000, with quite a large number of donors?
W Yes.
CA Well, looking at page 3, in terms of the donations above the sum of $200, there are only two.
W Yes.
CA Well, the balance then - well, the $4,500 attributed to those two people, the total is just under $14,000, leaves about $8,500. How was that derived?

(I think that actually leaves about $9,500. With maths like that, Mr Rice might have had an alternative career as a journalist or perhaps follow in the footsteps of another lawyer, a former Treasurer of Australia.)

W I had a campaign launch in early March which was —
CA Of 2016?
W Of 2016.
CA Right.
W And those funds were raised at that campaign launch.
CA Was that at a soccer club?

W Correct.

CA Can you explain what it consisted of?

W Yes. I had not a lot to do with the organisation. It was actually suggested by Bryan Galvin that I have a campaign launch. My response was that I thought I was a bit too occupied with the campaign. He suggested that he would assist, so we went from there and the local soccer club made itself available to host a meet and greet, just for a couple of hours, come along, hear from the Mayor, hear from a couple of my supporters and myself.

CA Which soccer club was that?

W Albany Creek Excelsior Soccer Club.

CA Were there a lot of people in attendance?

W There were.

CA You were aware, were you, Mr Charlton, of the requirement under the Electoral Act to keep a dedicated account for campaign purposes?

W Correct.

CA Did you do so?

W Yes, I did.

CA Can I show you this account statement. Is that a copy of a National Bank statement of yours?

W Yes, it is.

CA Is that account your dedicated campaign account?

W I believe so, yes.

CA We see in that, on the 8th of March, a cash deposit of $8,000. Do you see that?

W Yes, I do.

CA Can you just tell us where that was derived from?
W That was from the campaign launch.
CA Proceeds of the campaign launch?
W Correct.
CA Right. Can you tell us if that amount of $8,000 is included in the $13,900 that you declared as gifts?
W I would expect so.
CA Well, by what means was $8,000 raised on that occasion?
W It was $50 entry fee.
CA Yes.
W Off the top of my head there was around 90-odd people there and there were raffles run on the day.
CA And drinks as well?
W Sorry?
CA Drinks? Alcohol?
W Yes, there were, yes.
CA Just a couple of things, Mr Charlton, about the soccer club campaign launch that you mentioned.
W Yes.
CA Were there costs associated with the conduct of that?
W Yes, there were.
CA What were they?
W I have no idea. I didn't handle any of the money on the day. Bryan Galvin did all that. As I said, it was in the middle of the election campaign, so I had no role in that at all.
CA Do you know what sort of costs would have been incurred, or the cost to use the clubhouse, for example?

W I'm not in a position to comment. I didn't have any involvement with that on the day and that is now some time ago. As I said, I was in the middle of the election campaign.

CA Do we take it that it was arranged by others?

W I spoke to the soccer club, or the past president of the soccer club about it, but most of the organisation was done by others from my recollection, from my memory.

CA What others? Who were they?

W Bryan Galvin and a gentleman called Claude Sorbello, who was the past president of the soccer club.

CA So the logistics of getting food and drink and whatever else you had on the night were left to others?

W Correct.

CA You don't know how they were paid for?

W I assume they were paid out of the takings of the entrance fees.

CA Do you know who collected the entrance fees?

W I think it was Bryan, but I'm not 100 per cent sure.

CA Was it done in cash on the night or in some other way?

W No, it was cash.

CA It was a cash event, was it?

W To the best of my understanding, yes, it was.

CA And you received, at the end of the process, $8,000 as we have seen credited to your bank account?

W No, that was one payment. There is another payment there as well, sir.

CA Is there? Just point that out if you still have it in front of you.

W I think it's – to the best of my recollection, it's the $1455 on the 22nd of March and, again, Bryan handled all the finances and gave me the first deposit and said that they were still finalising costs and accounts, and then he gave me the balance which I deposited in the account.

CA That is Mr Charlton's evidence.

PO Thank you. Just finally the soccer club, were you a member of that club?

W No.

PO Were you a frequenter of the club?

W Infrequently. More upon invitation from the club to certain matches or specific events.

PO Did you expect that there would be a charge for you to use the club for a couple of hours for your launch?

W Correct.

PO Okay. There was no suggestion it was going to be given to you for nothing?

W No.

PO All right. Thank you.

11

ON TRANSPARENCY INTERNATIONAL'S global corruption index, Australia dropped from 8th spot in 2012 to 13th in 2015, a position it maintained in 2016. The Corruption Perceptions Index 2016 was released in January, 2017.

Peruvian lawyer José Carlos Ugaz is chair of Transparency International. In 2008, Mr Ugaz said corruption hurts all countries including those higher ranked such as Australia. In higher-scoring countries, he said, the situation might seem less obvious in the daily lives of citizens, but closed-door deals, illicit finance, and patchy law enforcement exacerbated many forms of corruption.

'We do not have the luxury of time,' said Mr Ugaz, handing down the latest 2016 report card. 'Corruption needs to be fought with urgency, so that the lives of people across the world improve.'

Given the recent Australian tax fraud scandal, attacks by some politicians and media on retiring Australian Human Rights Commission president Professor Gillian Triggs, the Commonwealth Bank money laundering, and CCC Operation Belcarra, the prospects of Australia rising higher on the corruption index in 2017 are not looking good. More doors have closed on dodgy business.

When I was reporting regularly on Pine Rivers Shire Council meetings, I was frustrated by the number of closed sessions. Before the sessions were closed I would let my feelings be known to the 10 councillors gathered around the impressive wooden table.

The councillors would always, and I do mean always, argue they had no choice but to close the meeting. I would scoff at that. It must have been a funny picture with the councillors playing hide-bound determinists and me arguing the voluntarist position.

Mayoral candidate Allan Sutherland was befriending me, a mild-mannered reporter of the community press, before the 2008 election of the inaugural Moreton Bay Regional Council. I spoke with Mr Sutherland about my annoyance with Pine Rivers Shire Council over the closed meetings. He said Redcliffe City Council rarely closed meetings. During his terms of office as Moreton Bay Mayor, closed sessions have become commonplace.

Most items on the huge project of a Petrie university have been discussed in closed session. An agreement between council and the University of the Sunshine Coast underpins the project on which Council expended $50 million to buy the university site. Council and the Sunny Coast uni withheld the agreement from ratepayers on the basis its contents were 'commercial-in confidence'.

The usual Council excuse for breaching the public right to know goes like this: 'Pursuant to s275 (1) of the Local Government Regulation 2012, clause (h), as the matter involves other business for which a public discussion would be likely to prejudice the interests of the Council or someone else, or enable a person to gain a financial advantage.'

When you read section 275 (1) you see the context of the philosophical debate I had with Pine Rivers Shire Councillors before they kicked me out of the chamber to hold their closed session.

S275 (1) reads: 'A local government or committee may resolve that a meeting be closed to the public if its councillors or members consider it necessary to close the meeting.'

You see the deterministic word 'necessary' which supports the councillors' point they had to close the meeting. But you also see the voluntarist words 'may' and 'consider'. It is two to one in my favour Ha ha, I win; isn't that how the law works?

I have already mentioned how obsessive Moreton Bay Council has been about keeping secret the details on the proposed Petrie University campus or the Mill at Moreton Bay, to give it its fancy title.

The Coordination Committee meeting on July 25 2017 closed a session to consider confidential item CI 'confidential the Mill at Moreton Bay – procurement of fill material.' The basis of confidentiality was, 'Pursuant to s275 (1) of the Local Government Regulation s12, clause (e), as the matter involves contracts proposed to be made by the Council.'

In the context of the CCC hearing, many residents might argue that matters involving Council contracts were items they would like to hear discussed in a public session.

Section 275 (1) is a real grab-all and a session can be closed because of: '(g) any action to be taken by the local government under the Planning Act, including deciding applications made to it under that Act; or (h) other business for which a public discussion would be likely to prejudice the interests of the local government or someone else, or enable a person to gain a financial advantage.'

The section could easily be abused by power brokers within a Council to exclude the public from hearing discussions which might not present that Council in a positive light. Councillors who value transparency should think four times whether closing a council meeting to the public is really necessary.

The Operation Belcarra report handed down on October 4 2017 made a point on conflict of interest which I consider equally pertinent to closed sessions.

'When government officials have poorly guided discretionary powers, the resulting lack of certainty can lead to perceived corruption and reduced public confidence,' the report read.

This is certainly the perception of Moreton Bay Council watchers dismayed by the frequency of closed sessions.

The public and the media are totally excluded from the unofficial decision making forums of workshops where a number of delegated councillors and public servants nut out motions to be put to the co-ordination committee. Council public meetings are rarely forums of robust debate as sittings of State and Federal Government often are. An astute betting person would put money on a resolution evolved at a workshop being passed at a co-ordination-committee meeting.

When my colleague, Walter Burns, and I were investigating Moreton Futures Trust we were most interested in a workshop where it appeared the recommendation of an outside consultant was rejected. In 2016, Moreton Bay Regional Councillors were warned it was a serious offence to talk with the general public or media about what happened at workshops. Workshops might include thought bubbles and drizzles from brainstorms best kept from the public. But, at the very least, workshops should be minuted and the minutes should be made public. All committee meetings should be held in public. Yes, even the financial ones; some would say, especially the financial ones.

My understanding is development applications in Ipswich also involved private meetings in a process not explained at the CCC hearings. A weekly meeting of an Ipswich Council board would include senior staff and the councillor chair of the planning committee.

The agenda included all applications received during the previous week and summaries of discussions between developers and staff on all major proposals.

The agenda would be sent out to all councillors over a number of days for their consideration. The board would consider councillors' feedback and raise issues of concern to staff by a set of notes.

It is understood the comments raised by the board were to be either followed or assessing staff would have to provide good reasons for not following them.

On the Gold Coast, the Mayoral Technical Advisory Committee (MTAC) meets in private at unminuted gatherings deriving planning policy. Developers dominate MTAC membership.

Brian Battersby, who retired in 2016 after forty years on Moreton Bay and Pine Rivers Councils, said to me the Moreton Bay Regional Council he served on was the best because there was no dissension. At the other end of the phone, I did not disagree but I shook my head sadly.

Before the amalgamation, councils had renegades. The late Christine Monsour on Pine Rivers Shire Council was legendary as was Lyn Devereaux on Caboolture Shire Council. The barneys between Redcliffe Mayor Allan Sutherland and Cr Peter Houston spilled over into threats of legal action and mutual referrals to the Crime and Misconduct Commission. Debates were not always edifying but they were passionate and committed. They also brought council meetings to the front pages of local newspapers which I considered a good thing.

I used to roll my eyes at some of the erratic logic of the late Ms Monsour. But I came to view it a shame she lost office at the 2008 election.

12

DEPUTY MAYOR OF IPSWICH CITY Paul Tully was editor of the University of Queensland student newspaper *Semper Floreat* in 1972, the year I began studying there. I don't recall having any personal interaction with him but my memory was of him as a member of Young Labor or the Labor Club.

I had more empathy with the radical students who seemed to be in a fierce battle of ideas with Mr Tully. The rads called him 'Spy' Tully as they suspected he was taking news of their meetings and activities to the administration.

Mr Tully's earlier thrust into the public limelight was as a first-year UQ student in 1969. He became the world potato-crisp eating champion chomping through 30 packets of crisps in 24 minutes 33.6 seconds without having a drink.

The Vice-Chancellor at the time was Zelman Cowen. Many of us students called him Zelmo. Word probably got back to him of the honorific but I don't know if he appreciated it. You think he would have as it sounds like the name of an academic super-hero. Zelmo! Faster than a speeding ballast! Zelmo! More powerful than a circumlocution! Zelmo!

The rads demanded a meeting with Zelmo at the drop of a hat. They had lots of grievances, none of which I can remember. Because the rads were invariably suspended from uni and did not want to be expelled they would appoint random first-years to be part of the deputation to take demands to Zelmo. I was chosen to be in one such delegation. All I remember of the meeting was when Zelman Cowen spoke to his personal assistant, the late Dr Robert Wensley. 'Get me a glass of water, Bob,' Zelmo said.

Zelman Cowen later became Governor-General of Australia and afterwards received the knighthood which seemed to be the done thing for ex G-Gs in those days. Zelmo ended up on the board of Fairfax Newspapers and even became chairman. I never worked for Fairfax so I did not have any call to reminisce with him about the good old days of UQ '72. Bob Wensley went on to have a distinguished academic and legal career after his days of water toting were gone.

In 1972, I crossed paths with another person destined to become a Governor-General. Dame Quentin Alice Louise Bryce was one of my law tutors in my legal career which spanned six months of 1972. I remember Ms Bryce as being pleasant and encouraging though I had the impression we both knew the law was not for me.

I think Mr Tully ran for editor of *Semper Floreat* again in 1973. If he did, he was beaten by the more radical Alan Knight who went on to have a distinguished career in journalism and academia. Mr Tully on the other hand became an Ipswich City Councillor at the age of 27 and continued uninterrupted in that role to this day.

An amusing article showing the interaction of independent young thinkers and university administration appeared in a 1973 edition of *Semper Floreat* during Mr Knight's tenure as editor. The 1973 feature story comments on an incident in 1971.

'CONTENT OF SECURITY OFFICER'S MEMO
Memorandum to: H.B. Green, Assistant Registrar University of Queensland.

At 1.20pm on the 3rd August, 1971, l observed a man known to me as William Steer writing on the door of the JD Story room in chalk the words 'Work you bastards'. He then chalked the words 'Work you bastards' on the door adjacent to the JD Story door.

I said to him, "That's not a nice thing to do, writing on the door."

He said, "Do you work?"

I said, "I do."

He said, "If the cap fits wear it."

He then walked out of the building to the front steps of the Union building where on the top step was a large bundle of the July issue of *Semper Floreat*. He picked up twelve to eighteen of the *Semper Floreat* and the chap with him said, "You can't take those", to which he replied, "I am taking them with me to Toowoomba. The match starts at 3 o'clock." He also called out from the stairway in a loud tone of voice, "Work you bastards, work."

- A.J. Sharp, Security Officer University of Queensland

Editorial comment in 1973:

Whilst the content of this excerpt from the Administration file on Will Steer is amusing, the following points should be noted:

1. This excerpt is only a small part of a very large file on Steer. Other contributors to it include not only Admin employees such as Sam Rayner (Registrar), Bruce Green (Assistant Registrar), and Bob (the students' friend) Wensley, but also, significantly, Union employees such as Mr Burns and Mr Armstrong.

2. All Admin files are classified, but some, notably those of student radicals, get special treatment under the specific control of the Registrar himself. These are kept under lock and key in a separate room.

3. The incident occurred within the walls of the student controlled student Union, where Steer was working in his own rather eccentric way against the Springboks. The match at Toowoomba to which he refers was one where anti-apartheid demonstrations took place and where Steer was subsequently arrested for his part in them.

4. Will Steer has never been a student at this University.'

(Semper Floreat, Vol. 43 No. 5, 1973, Page 1)

Will Steer was a 54-year-old man in 1971. In 1967, the Southport resident had stood for Mayor under the banner of *I Will Steer the Gold Coast*. He was arrested during the campaign.

Police alleged William Steer, then 50, damaged a white Pontiac Parisienne being used by Mayor Ern

Harley by pouring an offensive-smelling substance into it.

A council officer reported seeing Steer walking away from the mayoral car carrying a half-gallon ice cream can.

Police searched Steer's panel van and found an ice-cream can. Steer said he used it to carry cream and honey but the can when opened contained rotting prawns and a foul liquid.

(Coincidentally, or perhaps not, before becoming Mayor, Mr Harley owned a fish and chip shop. *Harley Seafood Take Away* at Labrador exists to this day.)

Steer later admitted to police to spilling some of the contents of the ice-cream can into the mayoral car but claimed it was accidental. Steer said, 'I am a man of God and I would not do anything malicious, even though Mr Harley has been very nasty in some of his remarks about me.'

Steer was found not guilty.

Will Steer was obviously one of those larger than life but otherwise ordinary Australians who find their places in the sun in protest movements. He is the sort of person deserving of a full length biography though none has been written.

His arrest at the Toowoomba rugby match was during a two-week strike by Queensland university students and staff in July/August 1971 against the South African rugby tour, the declaration of a State of Emergency by the Queensland Government, apartheid in South Africa, and racism in Australia.

Strike historian Roger Stuart said students dubbed Steer 'the Bishop' and King Yippee and were fond of the eccentric who sometimes stayed at the uni with his dog, Bark.

The strike committee received an injunction to quit their campaign headquarters in the JD Story room one cold winter Wednesday. They decided to risk arrest although they were warned police might evict them overnight. Roger Stuart reported, 'The night passed in paranoid speculation about the extent of likely police brutality, about what to do if they came, and by continual acts of outrage by Will Steer (e.g. turning on the fans at 3am) who sought to "keep everyone on their toes".'

Inevitably critics and sections of the media denigrated the unlikely renegade Will Steer as a 'paid outside agitator', a description which the protestors made fun of by giving him the honorific, POA. Roger Stuart and other protestors discovered the real puppet master behind Will Steer.

'Finally the horrible truth was revealed. It was Will Steer who was the arch manipulator. Then another more sinister truth was revealed . . . Will Steer's dog was in fact manipulating him. 'Bark', a white dog had no interest in combatting racism, and had in fact, at the right moment, pissed on the carpet and set in motion the chain of events leading to the injunctions and the possibilities of police on campus (carpet had to be shampooed etc.). He then planned to use the chaos to ride to absolute power in true Napoleonic fashion. 'Bark' was leading the first

significant movement on this campus for white dog power! Bark had Will Steer on a leash!'
Semper Floreat (Vol. 41 No. 11) 1st September 1971

In 2017, groups across Queensland are standing up for reform of local government and they are being criticised in general by authorities and sections of the media with certain members being called out as Will Steer was. One reform group gathering I was at responded with humour to their critics and I am sure that will be a continuing tactic.

One hundred and eighteen people voted for William Aabraham-Steer at the Southport by-election of June 20, 1987. Former Queensland and Australian rugby-league player Mick Vievers won the seat when 7164 people voted for him. Mick Vievers has a road named after him.

Robert E Lee stood for Labor and there is no statue of him on the Gold Coast.

In those days, positions on ballot papers were placed in alphabetical order of surnames. This probably explains the deliberately misspelt addition of Abraham to Bishop Will Steer's surname. This method of ballot order carried on for many years though it was known to encourage 'donkey' candidates with low-alphabet names who were enlisted to preference other candidates they were associated with. Unfair practices can be tolerated for a long time in political administration. A continuing example of this is the physical how-to-vote leaflet, an environmentally unfriendly object, handed out by candidates and their supporters. The practice persists because major parties and incumbents can get more people to hand them out on polling day.

For some time now, positions on ballot papers have been selected by random draws.

In the mid 1990s I began work for *Big Rigs* newspaper, part of the historic Ipswich based *Queensland Times* newspaper group. I interviewed Councillor Paul Tully for the flagship *Queensland Times* once or twice during election campaigns. To be honest he was best known to all us journalists for his habit of always racing to the far left of a group being photographed. This did not signify a radicalisation of his politics. If you stand to the left, you are to the camera's right and will end up in the eye-catching position in a published photo.

After Ipswich Mayor Paul Pisasale (pronounced Pis-ar-lee) resigned, and was later charged with corruption, extortion and other offences, Acting Mayor Cr Tully said he would put up his hand for the permanent job. Cr Tully said he had had little to do with the city's developers.

As it turned out Cr Tully won the opinion polls, leading up to the election but lost the one that counted.

Former policeman, 17-year Ipswich councillor, and Labor Party member, running as an independent, Andrew Antoniolli, defeated fellow Labor Party member, running as an independent, Cr Tully for the mayoral job at the by-election of August 19, 2017.

Cr Antoniolli might be considered a newbie compared to Cr Tully who had 38-years straight in council. Being deputy mayor under Paul Pisasale might have hindered Cr Tully in some quarters.

Also Cr Tully probably made a critical blunder when he failed to declare who had paid for two billboards within seven business days of the billboards going up. This was the first local government election where the new disclosure laws were in place. Although his law degree is probably gathering dust in a cupboard somewhere, Cr Tully was probably right when he said the donation only had to be declared within seven business days of receipt. He did not elaborate but the loophole was obvious enough: if a donor makes a pledge and a candidate thinks it is solid, they can spend money without declaring the donor. Even if Mr Tully was correct, he seemed to me to be waving at the crowd as he drove through a loophole. To my mind, it was not a good look. How law-makers did not anticipate the loophole must make observers shake their heads.

During his campaign, Cr Antoniolli said it was silly to expect him to know about Mayor Pisasale's alleged dodgy activity.

Mr Antoniolli ran on promises of transparency of council decisions and an audit of council-owned companies, controversially set up by Cr Pisasale. These private companies did not have as tight disclosure provisions as Ipswich Council had.

Cr Antoniolli espoused zero tolerance for illegal activity and promised co-operation with the CCC after the commission charged Ipswich Works, Parks, and Recreation Chief Operating Officer Craig Maudsley on September 12, 2017. Mr Maudsley, who retained the presumption of innocence, allegedly tried to gain a contractual benefit for a council subcontractor while unfairly causing financial detriment to Colmine Consulting.

Ipswich CEO Jim Lindsay contacted the 1200 council staff to confirm illegality would not be tolerated. 'The Mayor (Cr Antoniolli) has made it quite clear that there is zero tolerance when it comes to illegal activity,' Mr Lindsay said. 'That has always been then case and always will be.' The next day CCC officers arrested Mr Lindsay on charges of official corruption. Cr Antoniolli described Mr Lindsay's arrest as a shock.

Mr Lindsay became CEO after previous CEO Carl Wulff (July 2006 –December 2013) resigned when he was the subject of a CMC inquiry. The inquiry was referred to the Ipswich Council which decided not to take action.

Mr Wulff became CEO at Liverpool Council in Sydney where he was at the centre of an asbestos scandal in 2016. Unkind Western Sydney Liverpudlians dubbed him the Wulff of George Street, the substitute for Wall Street being the main thoroughfare. Council minutes show he resigned in March but these minutes were retracted and Mr Wulff's Linkedin entry shows he limped on until July 2016. But he was gone before then, if not officially, as by May, Michael Cullen was acting CEO.

In September 2016, Liverpool Council investigated the ex CEO's involvement in locking in the Council to a 10-year deal with Propel Partnerships, an administrative-services company majority owned by the Local Government Association of Queensland. Mr Wulff was CEO at Ipswich Council when that Council signed a contract with Propel.

In May, 2016, a fraudster, hearing of Mr Wulff's woes at Liverpool, set up the fake Facebook Page *Carl Wulff for Mayor of Ipswich*. Proving once again, truth is stranger than fiction, Mr Wulff did return to the Ipswich area and ended up handing out how-to-vote cards for successful 2017 by-election mayoral candidate Cr Antoniolli.

Maybe he should have stayed away. In October, 2017, CCC officers arrested and charged Mr Wulff, 65, of Brookwater, with official corruption and attempting to pervert the course of justice. His wife Sharon Oxenbridge, 50, was also charged with corruption.

Even a casual observer of Australian councils will know there is a Travelling CEO Show for chief executives who fall out of favour or leave under a cloud, which might be completely unjustified, only to arrive at another council. Australia, it's a big country, with a small pool of people, usually men, of CEO material. Pack up the diaries and grab the old sunnies; it's the CEO Salvation Show.

After losing the mayoral by-election, still deputy, Cr Tully, had a re-think of his glowing references for

Mr Pisasale. He told the state newspaper councillors were suspicious of Mayor Pisasale's party lifestyle and business associates. But, Cr Tully said, Mr Pisasale was a winner who stressed not displaying disunity in public. Cr Tully said this winning formula meant no sitting councillor was voted out of office for 16 years after 2000. To lose one councillor may be regarded as a misfortune but to lose none looks like carefulness.

Cr Tully was a witness at the Operation Belcarra public hearing immediately before Mike Charlton on Wednesday, April 19, 2017.

On the whole, Mr Tully was erudite and philosophical but he offered some Pythonesque comic relief when it was revealed he had two bank accounts processing campaign donations.

CA (Mr Rice) So that's a deposit by him of $2,000; correct?
W (Cr Tully) Yes, yes.
CA Is that a donation?
W Oh, yes, it was.
CA But not to the Goodna Community Fund, can I suggest; it was a campaign donation to you, wasn't it?
W No, it went directly into the Goodna Community Fund.
CA To be applied to what purpose?
W Applied to my campaign.
CA Did you understand that to be a donation by that gentleman to your election campaign?
W No.

CA Well, what was it?
W It was a donation to the Goodna Community Fund.

Cr Tully favours banning developer donations and the Labor Party member wants political affiliation of all candidates declared. He says he has always made his political affiliations known and, to be fair, the public should be aware of all candidates' affiliations, not just those of sitting councillors who declare allegiances in their interests register.

I have problems with this. At a practical level, how do you determine political affiliation beyond party membership? Moreton Bay Councillor Mike Charlton said he has never been a party member yet he was funded in 2008 to the tune of $20,000 by a trust linked to the Liberal Party which later that year joined with the National Party to form the LNP. Mayor Allan Sutherland twice ran for state office for the Liberal Party but says he has long severed his ties with the LNP. Logan City Mayor Luke Smith said he was an LNP member for three years, and his current interests register shows no political affiliation.

There is also a point I made earlier. Elected candidates deserve closer scrutiny. Given the scarce resources available to the scrutineers – the ECQ, media and the public – the elected who can intervene to bestow favours are the ones who must be watched closely.

Recommendation 3 of the October 2017 Operation Belcarra report requested that laws be enacted compelling all candidates to complete an interests register including membership of political parties and trade associations (read unions.) There is a danger here that voters are being encouraged to discriminate against candidates based on party or union membership and I hope the State Government strikes out this recommendation. I have already raised other issues about party affiliation versus membership and unnecessary intrusion into the affairs of candidates who will nearly all lose. As I have said, I am in favour of interests registers for winning candidates.

    I would prefer internet space to be provided for each candidate to declare their policies and whatever interests they choose to disclose. I might declare my membership of the NLP, the Neo Luddite Party. You would love our monthly meetings where we reverse our FJ Holdens over hills of laptop computers.

    For reasons I will elaborate on later, I would prefer political parties to contest local government elections but I know I am in a minority on that. Paradoxically, as a number of commentators have pointed out, voters don't hold political affiliation against candidates. The Pauls – Tully and Pisasale – both regularly received more than 80 per cent of the vote, meaning many conservative voters at the state and federal level voted for these two members of the Labor Party (though not Party candidates) for Ipswich Council. Voters just don't consider party affiliation such a big deal when voting at council level so why should we make a big deal of it for candidates.

Let's just remind sitting councillors that history shows they have a significant advantage over new contenders so they really cannot complain about a slightly uneven playing field when it comes to declarations of political allegiance.

As LGAQ CEO Greg Hallam says good public policy is 'one that you can enforce and one that improves the system.' I doubt if candidates declaring political affiliation meets either of those criteria.

Transcript #7
Abridged by Bernie Dowling

Witness Councillor Paul Tully, April 19, 2017
PO, Presiding Officer Alan MacSporran QC
CA, Counsel Assisting, Glen Rice QC
W, Witness Councillor Paul Tully
CCC hearing conducted at Fortitude Valley, Brisbane

CA Sir, is your name Paul Gregory Tully?
W That's correct.
CA You are the councillor for Division 2 of Ipswich City Council?
W Yes.
CA You're also Deputy Mayor?
W Yes.
CA You are, I think, the longest-serving councillor in Queensland?
W In Queensland, but I did find someone in South Australia who's got 40 years up.
CA Are you going for the record?

W He said he can't remember when he was elected, so I thought, well, I don't want to get to that stage.
CA Thirty-seven years, I think, in your case, is it?
W Thirty-eight.
CA You were very successful at the last election?
W Yes.
CA What percentage of vote, Mr Tully?
W 82.5 per cent.
CA Is that consistent with previous results, because you've been around a long time?
W It's not the highest I've ever received. The highest was in 2008. I got 87 per cent.
CA You're a Labor Party member, aren't you?
W Yes.
CA For how long have you been a member?
W I joined in 1975. So that's 42 years.
CA As a sitting councillor, as you have been for such a long time, is that membership something that's declared in a formal way?
W Yes, it is. It's on the register of interests on which all sitting members in Queensland, local government councillors, have to declare membership of political parties.
CA Is that the register maintained by the Ipswich City Council?
W Yes, maintained by the CEO, that's right. That's publicly available on the internet.
CA Do I understand correctly that's separate from what records the Electoral Commission may keep?
W That's correct, yes.

CA Is there any such requirement for a candidate who is not a sitting councillor to make public, for example, their party membership for campaign purposes?

W No. No, not at all.

CA It would be fair to say, I think, you would claim to know your electorate very well?

W Yes.

CA Is alignment of that kind something that electors want to know, in your view?

W Absolutely, people would want to know if you're a member of a political party. In my case, that has been something that has been known for many, many years, often commented on in the local press and media, about my particular membership. But since 2000, the Labor Party has taken the decision not to endorse candidates in Ipswich and other provincial areas, so that we have, in a formal way, no connection with the Labor Party except for being an individual member.

CA I take it you would also say that if a candidate was receiving financial support from a party, that was something that electors have an interest in knowing?

W Absolutely, and I assume it –

CA Prior to casting a vote?

W Yes.

CA You know about the disclosure returns –

W Yes.

CA - which the Electoral Commission requires?

W Yes.

CA You know that they are completed after the event?

W Yes.

CA After the election. What's your view about whether they serve their purpose in making disclosure to electors?

W Well, I believe there should be real-time disclosure of local government expenditure. I believe there's a Bill before the parliament in relation to that. It applies to state members at the moment, state candidates at the moment. I think it would be an opportunity for the community to be aware of that and possibly other things as well.

(The state bill was extended to local government elections, perhaps to Mr Tully's disadvantage when he ran for Mayor in the by-election, as I have suggested above in regard to who paid for Cr Tully's two billboards.

At least Cr Tully retains his councillor's job after the by-election. If a sitting councillor runs for mayor at a regular election, they cannot run for a seat as well. This rule though sensible provides additional protection for a mayor to retain office.)

If you look at the conflict of interests form, which needs to be lodged, there's a whole range of other things – membership of companies, shareholdings, landholdings and things like that. There's probably a broader range of issues that should be disclosed. At the moment, it's not a level playing field. If you're a sitting councillor, you must disclose your membership. If you're a candidate, you don't have to.

CA The subject of donations from property developers cropped up before your arrival.

W Yes.

CA What are the risks that you see are associated with property developers donating to councillors?

W I think the risks are the familiarity and certainly in the community's mind a perception that property developers, active property developers, are donating for one reason.

CA Would you accept donations from a property developer?

W Yes, but –

CA Have you done?

W Yes, and I've rejected them as well, as recently as the 2016 election. Up until 2016, I was the chair of the planning and development committee. Most of the applications are done under delegation. The last figures I saw, there were about 900 applications in a preceding year. I'm not sure if that was a calendar year or a financial year. Only about four went to a council meeting. The rest were determined by officers under delegation. I just have a view, in dealing with those situations, that developers are putting forward their interests, their personal interests, which often don't coincide with the community's interests.

(My understanding of the historical processing of Ipswich development applications is that there was more councillor involvement than Cr Tully's explanation suggests.)

CA You mentioned, I think, in the course of your answer that donations from property developers can give rise to a perception that there may be some conflict?

W Oh, I think that would be a widespread view in the community. That's why my view is – and I've expressed this previously – that Queensland should follow the New South Wales model of banning all donations from property developers to both state and federal candidates in that state, and that's something I think should happen here.

(The Operation Belcarra report Recommendation 20 asked that all donations from property developers and their agents be banned. Queensland Premier Annastacia Palaszczuk said the Government would introduce such a ban for State and Local Government elections. She needed to win an election on November 25, 2017, before she could do that. That election might be known as The Developers' Last Resort.)

CA Would you go further and favour a system that bans all donations?

W No, I wouldn't support that, but I do believe there are some – the corollary of that would be that there should be public funding of local government campaigns. That would significantly reduce the reliance on any donations. It would also mean that the donations would be limited. There would be probably a more equal, level playing field.

CA We've been speaking about perception. Could you give us your insight into where that perception developed or how that perception is managed within the conduct of council business?

W Well, it's not so much perception. It's the requirements to disclose if one has a material personal interest or a conflict of interest. A material personal interest is probably easier to determine. Conflicts of interest can be sometimes difficult to judge. When matters come up to committee, the only requirement by law to disclose the conflicts is either at a committee meeting of the council or at a council meeting.

CA How satisfactorily does all that work, in your view?

W My own view is that if it's already on the register, it probably shouldn't have to be disclosed again, but other people take a different view.

(I certainly take a different view. How do ratepayers or the media monitor councillors under the preferred Paul-Tully system? Check every councillor's register against every vote? It is more logical, efficient, and fairer for each councillor to do the cross-check of their register and agenda items?

Governance should be regarded as part of a councillor's job not a tiresome burden.

A CCC recommendation is that, after other reforms promoting education, a councillor should be deemed to be aware of all conflicts of interest. In other words it is up to a councillor to do their homework.)

CA Mr Tully, you would be aware of the requirement in the Local Government Electoral Act to maintain a dedicated bank account for campaign purposes?
W Yes.
CA Did you have such an account for the 2016 elections?
W Yes.
CA In what name?
W I think it was in my name and my wife's name.
CA Is that an account styled as PG & LS Tully?
W Yes, with the Bendigo Bank.
CA Could you tell us, Mr Tully, what is the Goodna Community Fund?
W Yes. That was an account that was set up in 2008 after a house fire in Goodna where a three-year-old boy died in the fire, and it has been used, I think, on four occasions over those years for small donations probably averaging no more than about $500 on each occasion.
CA You established that fund?
W Yes, myself and my wife, yes.
CA You and your wife opened a bank account styled PG & LS Tully Goodna Community Fund; is that right?
W Oh, I thought it was just Goodna Community Fund.
CA I've got a bank statement here. I'll show it to you.
W Okay, yes. But we're individual signatories to it. It could be operated by either.

CA   Could I just ask you about some of those transactions. First is a deposit of a cheque for $2,000. Do you have any recollection of that?
W   Yes, that was a cheque from a Jim McIlmurray, who owns a business at Redbank.
CA   So that's a deposit by him of $2,000; correct?
W   Yes, yes.
CA   Is that a donation?
W   Oh, yes, it was.
CA   But not to the Goodna Community Fund, can I suggest; it was a campaign donation to you, wasn't it?
W   No, it went directly into the Goodna Community Fund.
CA   To be applied to what purpose?
W   Applied to my campaign.
CA   Did you understand that to be a donation by that gentleman to your election campaign?
W   No.
CA   Well, what was it?
W   It was a donation to the Goodna Community Fund.
CA   But you wouldn't suggest that this donation was in support of some tragedy that had occurred?
W   No, no. Not at all. No, not at all. It was clearly encompassed by what Joan Sheldon had said, to separate yourself from the day-to-day routine of the receipt of donations and the expenditure of campaign moneys.

(Joan Sheldon, a name which kept cropping up, without any notion of impropriety, was the female equivalent of Third Man, Bryan Galvin 'There was a third woman. She didn't give evidence.'

Ms Sheldon, employed by the LGAQ to explain ethical electioneering, was a Liberal MP from 1990 to 2004. She was Deputy Premier from 1996-98. A physiotherapist before entering parliament, Ms Sheldon was State Attorney-General for a week in a transition government.)

CA But you have to have a dedicated account, Mr Tully, to receive such things?

W Yes, which I have.

13

FOR SOME REASON my report on the evidence of Mayor Allan Sutherland did not make the electronic media of the next day.
Never fear, here is what I wrote:

MORETON Bay Regional Council Mayor Allan Sutherland was asked about his political donations on Day 4 of the Crime and Corruption Commission (CCC) hearing into the 2016 council elections of Moreton Bay, the Gold Coast and Ipswich.

Councillor Sutherland received substantial donations from Moreton Futures Trust in 2012 and 2016.

The presiding officer at the inquiry is Alan MacSporran and Glen Rice is Counsel Assisting.

Councillor Sutherland said he was unaware of his legal obligations about knowing who the trustees of Moreton Futures Trust were.

Mr Rice asked, 'You really ought to have included the names of the trustees on your disclosure, Mr Sutherland, shouldn't you?'

'I found out that this week,' Cr Sutherland replied.

The Mayor did not know in 2012 who were the trustees who decided to give tens of thousands of dollars to his successful campaign.

He spoke to his wife Gayle about the trust. 'I remember saying to Gayle, "I think it's Bryan Galvin and all that business mob, whoever they are, but I said, (long-term Councillor) Brian Battersby and them say they're all really upstanding people."'

He did not find out Aspley doctor, John Ryan, had been a trustee until 2016.

This exchange between Mr Rice (CA) and Councillor Sutherland (W) backgrounds how:

W I had a particularly difficult health situation both before and during the election.
CA You consulted him for health reasons, did you?
W Well, he was recommended to me because . . .
CA I don't want to know about your health. That's private.

Cr Sutherland recalled a Moreton Futures Trust fundraiser in 2012 when he was asked to be a guest speaker. 'I was looking at all the people around the room, being new to the fold, a mayor that had only been there for four years, I didn't know a lot of the business community, so I was happy if we could raise the money this year (2016) without having fundraisers, as such.'

His 'very good mate' Redcliffe developer David Trask helped Moreton Futures Trust raised funds for 2012 and 2016.

But there was a risk, Councillor Sutherland said. 'If money went into Moreton Futures, I didn't know whether I was getting the whole, part, everything, and what other campaigns they were supporting.'

In 2016 Moreton Futures Trust gave more than $120,000 towards Cr Sutherland's successful mayoral bid.

Cr Sutherland said he offered to some sitting councillors the sharing of how to vote cards and billboards and he provided endorsement letters in 2016. 'I had candidates that weren't elected asking me to do joint How to Vote Cards with them, and I wouldn't do it, definitely because I thought that that would impact on the impartiality of me as Mayor.'

(I have read and re-read that last statement about the impartiality of only supporting incumbents but the logic continues to evade me.)

The sitting councillors who accepted and he were not members of a group.

'Most people looking at that by arrangement would see that as the sitting council, not a group,' Cr Sutherland said. 'There's fierce independence in our council, and it's probably the strength of the Moreton Bay Council.'

A LOOK AT THE VOTING RECORDS of councillors at the four Moreton Bay Regional Council co-ordination committee meetings of February 2017 gives a rough measure of the 'fierce independence in our council'. The co-ord meetings are where Council passes binding resolutions.

The meeting of February 7:

- carried item 1.1. The vote was 12-0.
- Item 3.1 was carried 12-0.
- Item 6.1 was carried 12-0.

Our running tally by meeting's end is 36-0. These figures are on the council website.

The February 14 meeting:
- carried Item 2.1 on votes 11-0;
- item 4.1 at 11-0,
- 5.1 at 11-0, and
- 6.1 at 11-0.

Is there any discernible pattern emerging in the deliberations of this fiercely independent council?

The other two items on February 14 were confidential which meant the public gallery was cleared and councillors met in closed session. The votes from the closed session were later disclosed to the public.

The basis of confidentiality for both motions was 'Pursuant to s275 (1) of the Local Government Regulation 2012, clause (h), as the matter involves other business for which a public discussion would be likely to prejudice the interests of the Council or someone else, or enable a person to gain a financial advantage.'

Motion C.1 was passed 11-0 and C.2 was passed with 10 councillors for and one against.

Our running tally after the February 14 meeting is 112 for and one against, 112-1

At the February 21 meeting, the nay-sayers really created an impression. (Rumour has it recalcitrant

Moreton Bay councillors in this fiercely independent council are berated as not being team players.)

- Item 2.1 was passed 10-2 and item 2.2 was passed 10-2. Is a revolution in embryo?
- Item 2.3 passed 13-0, item 3.1, 13-0; Item 4.1, 13-0; 6.1, 13-0 and confidential item C.1, 13-0.

Only 12 councillors voted for items 2.1 and 2.2 because Mayor Allan Sutherland removed himself from the chamber after declaring a perceived conflict of interest for each item. As it was a perceived only, he could have chosen to stay and even vote on the items.

Our running tally is now 197 votes for, five votes against, 197-5. The five against votes were recorded by two of the 13 councillors, Cr Denise Sims and Cr Brooke Savige.

February 28 was a quiet morning at the co-ordination committee. Only one item was voted on and passed 11-0.

Our final count for the fiercely independent council is 208-5. Eleven of the councillors recorded yes votes for the entire month.

As you can imagine, little public debate is held at co-ordination committee meetings on items passed unanimously. Closed meetings, of course, preclude open debate. Meetings are held on a Tuesday morning, when much of the adult population are at work. The meetings often take only a couple of hours, sometimes less than half an hour. They are not audio-visually recorded and hence not available as internet videos to those unable to attend the meeting.

Even the most dedicated of council watchers, who tend to be retirees, only attend co-ordination committee meetings irregularly, mainly to show councillors they are still watching. For the most part, the watchers diligently digest agendas before meetings and minutes after. Both are available on the internet.

Transcript #8
Abridged by Bernie Dowling

Witness Mayor Allan Sutherland, April 21, 2017
PO, Presiding Officer Alan MacSporran QC
CA, Counsel Assisting, Glen Rice QC
W, Witness Mayor Allan Sutherland

CA Sir, is your full name Allan Robert Sutherland?
W That's correct.
CA Mr Sutherland, you're the Mayor of Moreton Bay Regional Council; correct?
W That's also correct.
CA You were elected to that position in 2008?
W That's also correct.
CA Successfully contested elections in 2012 and 2016?
W I started in 1994 at Redcliffe.
CA Yes. You were the Mayor of Redcliffe at one time, before the amalgamation?
W Yes, that's correct.

CA Are you a member of a political party, Mr Sutherland?
W No.
CA Have you been?
W In the '90s, the first half of the '90s.
CA Have you been a member of any party whilst you've been Mayor of Moreton Regional Council?
No, not Moreton nor Redcliffe. I haven't had any political involvement with any party for almost two decades, I'd say.

(When Councillor Sutherland was running for mayor of Moreton Bay Region in 2008, he told me the Liberal Party promised him the world of support and gave him little at his two attempts in the early 1990s to win the state seat of Redcliffe.

Cr Sutherland likes to regard himself as a pragmatist dealing with both sides of the two-party dominated Australian politics. But at heart, he is a conservative. Indeed Moreton Bay Futures Trustee Kirby Leeke informed me his perception of Allan Sutherland as conservative was at the centre of the decision to help fund his campaign for mayor. We do not have a nominal Conservative Party in Australia where that role is filled by a coalition of Liberal and National Parties, and, in Queensland, by the merged LNP.)

CA Do you campaign as an independent?
W Absolutely.
CA What does that mean to you?
W It means that I have no political master, neither Labor or Liberal. I just don't have to answer. It gives

me a lot more freedom, as a Mayor, to be able to talk to state or federal colleagues, whether they be, as we've got at the moment, a state Labor Party and an LNP federal government.

(The Federal Government was actually a Coalition of the Liberal Party and the National Party in 2017. The Liberals and Nationals amalgamated in Queensland in 2008 to form the LNP.)

CA Candidates for local government elections are not party endorsed, are they, at least not in Moreton?

W No.

CA But some may over time have memberships of parties or other obvious signs of political affiliation?

W That's true, as we have in Moreton (Bay Regional) Council at the moment.

CA I think it's your view, is it not, that voters don't want party-endorsed candidates?

W Well, I'm sure voters don't want politics, be it of any persuasion, running their councils.

CA Why do you say that?

W Why do I say that?

CA Mmm.

W I think local government's parish pump politics. It's closest to the people. I don't think people want to see party involvement in their local councils. I have no objection to people belonging to political parties. We've sat with members of different political parties in my council, or our council, ever since it was formed in 2008 and my message is clear: keep your politics at the door.

CA So candidates do not have party funding for their campaigns?
W Not that I'm aware of, no.
CA You don't approve, either, do you, of unions supporting candidates financially?
W No, I don't. No.
CA I know you gave an example of that when you were interviewed by the Commission investigators.
W I have some examples here.
CA We probably don't need to go to them, but is it fair to say that you don't support party funding for candidates?

(Cr Sutherland turned up for the hearing, bearing a welter of information in folders. He looked like *Waiting for Godot*'s Lucky, bound down by bags.)

W Well, no, not – I guess the issue arises that the people don't know. And I think we had a perfect example in the last election, when people found out that a person was supported by a union in a fairly major way. It probably cost them the election. But had they have not found out that, they more than likely would have won that seat and I would have felt that that would have been by deception.

(I wonder how the people found out about candidate Kimberly James and the CMFEU's sponsorship which was a totally legal transaction.

Veteran Brisbane journalist, Roger Davis, struck by another bout of chronic empathy with Cr Sutherland, wrote about it before the 2016 election.

'Mayor Allan Sutherland has sounded alarm over a secret push by the nation's most militant union to gain influence in local councils.

'Sutherland, whose council enjoys good relations with more moderate unions, said he was surprised to learn the CFMEU was supporting Kimberley – sic, but it is Kimberly – James, a candidate in division three who was running as an independent.

"I was shocked. I was horrified," Sutherland said.'

SHOCK! HORROR! Those words must have brought a nostalgic tear to the eye of former editor, Roger Davis.)

CA In the absence of party funding, campaigns have to be funded somehow, don't they?

W It's terrible. Yes.

CA You say it's terrible? Well, to explore that –

W It's the worst nightmare.

CA Yes, okay. Candidates have to rely on their own resources or fundraisers or donations or a combination of it?

(Mr Rice appeared to grow a little testy at Cr Sutherland's fondness for hyperbole.)

W It depends on the size of the council. In the old Redcliffe Council, when I joined in '94, to the best of my memory virtually all of my campaigns were sole funded. Moreton Bay Region encompasses three federal electorates and some eight shared state seats. It's the third-largest council in Australia. To give an example, I've got two letterbox drops here. The postage for those was around the 45K mark.

CA A big impost on a candidate to fund their own campaign, is it?

W It's a $200,000 exercise, minimum.

CA That's at your level; correct?

W Mmm, yes.

CA But for the average councillor, less than that or not?

W Depending on the councillor. If you were someone like Brian Battersby, who was there for 40-odd years, he could probably do it on tuppence, he was so well known. If you were new to the fold and you didn't have a name and you had to establish a name, I suppose upwards to a polished, professional campaign, maybe $35,000 or $40,000.

(This is an exaggeration. There are 12 divisions so the total spend for 12 candidates would be upwards of $400,000 when Cr Sutherland says the required mayoral spend for that same area is $200,000.)

CA So did I sum it up correctly that candidates need to rely on personal funding, fundraisers or donations?

W Yes, I'd say that would be correct.

CA You described that as terrible, I think, a moment ago. Why do you say that, Mr Sutherland?

W It's the worst part of your job as a Mayor or a councillor. No-one likes it. I've never spoken to any Mayor anywhere at any time that likes fundraising activities. If you can pick a worst part of your job, that would be it. It's not pleasant.

CA Is there a better model, the Commission would be interested to know, in this context?

W Well, I think there needs to be changes, yes.
CA Do you have any suggestions?
W I've got a lot of suggestions. I think there should be caps.
CA I beg your pardon?
W There should be caps on the amount of donations. The public, quite rightfully, do get suspicious of donors, for different reasons. I made a prediction that I'm possibly the last independent Mayor of Moreton Bay Region. If we don't allow some funding somehow, particularly for mayoral candidates in the large amalgamated areas it will become the domain of political parties and unions, and I think that will be sad, or we'll have a whole roomful of mayors that are multimillionaires.

(As opposed to mayors whose campaigns are funded by multimillionaires.)

So what I'm saying is, I guess, in essence, there has to be some form of funding in some way, shape or form to run a successful mayoral candidacy campaign in a large region.

(Public funding of local government elections could provide an incentive to bring back party politics.)

CA Another issue is disclosure of donations.
W Yes.
CA You, for the purpose of your 2016 campaign, shared campaign material with a number of other candidates?
W Yes.
CA There were a number of How to Vote Cards?

W Yes.

CA You and other candidates used joint How to Vote Cards – or at least some candidates; correct?

W Yes.

CA We might have some examples here. I am just interested to know the extent to which that occurred, Mr Sutherland. There is one here. It appears to be a joint card with Councillor Julie Greer.

W I think I've got them probably all here. I think I've probably got every one of them here.

CA Is that a joint card that you used for the last election with Councillor Greer?

W Yes. I've got a copy of them all here.

CA I tender that. PO Exhibit 68.

(The card tendered was wrong. It was from 2012 not 2016. The correct card was later substituted.)

CA You shared another one with Councillor Houghton?

W Yes.

CA You shared another card with Councillor Gillam?

(Councillor Gillam is a staunch member of the Labor Party and, despite Cr Sutherland's avowal of independence, many in Labor are convinced the Mayor has conservative sympathies. He supported the LNP candidate who lost against Labor in the 2014 by-election for Redcliffe. I believe allowing Cr Sutherland to pay fully for the billboard displayed a lack of judgement on Cr Gillam's part.)

W That's correct.

CA You shared another How to Vote Card with Councillor Charlton?

W That's correct.
W Yes.
CA There was also another with Councillor Flannery; correct?
W Yes, that's correct.
CA How did that come about?
W Well, the councillors that I asked if they would want to do them, some said yes; some said no. There was no binding obligation on them. For instance, Koliana Winchester shared a billboard with us but didn't share a How to Vote Card with us.

(Koliana Winchester is also a member of the Labor Party and holds a council division in Redcliffe where the Mayor campaigned against Labor at the state level. I asked Cr Winchester about accepting the Mayor's offer of paying for the shared billboard. She was quite hostile, rebuking me for bringing politics into it.)

CA Did you discuss sharing of costs with the councillors concerned that you were sharing with?
W Yes, I did. I can't recall – we're going back 18 months ago. I can't recall which ones, but some councillors said, in the first instance, that they'd just go halves, and other councillors, I suggested – well, I suggested to them all that I'd try to make myself available through the campaign to pay for it, but –
CA All of it, you mean?
W Yes, but it must be declared. A couple of the councillors at the time said, no, they were happy to pay the costs, and, in the end, they said, "Well, if you're willing to pay the costs, yes, that will be okay."

CA So you paid the full cost for at least some of those?

W Yes, providing that it was fully declared.

(Think about this for a moment: the Mayor offers to pay part of councillors' campaign expenses and the fiercely independent six accept the offer.)

CA Can I suggest to you it's self-evident, really, that the How to Vote Cards do cross-promote the election prospects of both of you?

W I don't think you can really deny that they cross-promote, but I just don't know how you qualify or quantify it.

CA Did you hesitate, having made an arrangement with these councillors to do that, that the appearance of the How to Vote Cards as joint cards in each case could give rise to a view that, by arrangement, you had formed a group to support each other's election?

W No, I'd adopt the attitude that most people looking at that by arrangement would see that as the sitting council, not a group. They would see Mick Gillam and Allan Sutherland. They know Mick Gillam is their sitting councillor and Allan Sutherland is their Mayor. I wouldn't suggest it's a group as such but more as a council. They're the sitting councillors.

CA You had a selected – well, you had a number of councillors whose re-election you favoured; correct?

W Absolutely. And, conversely, I had candidates that weren't elected asking me to do joint How to Vote Cards with them, and I wouldn't do it, definitely because I thought that that would impact on the impartiality of me as Mayor and I didn't want to be seen to be influencing the outcome of a division.

CA Okay.

W But I don't mind doing it with a sitting councillor, particularly if we've got a respect for each other's ideals.

CA Billboards are a bit like the How to Vote Cards, aren't they? They involve a representation that you support each other for the purpose of election?

W Well, I wouldn't suggest that it was a – I would suggest it could be taken as support, yes, but it certainly – if you're on the same billboard together, it's support. But it's not – I wouldn't suggest it's a group as such.

CA Arising from all of that, I'll ask you again, from the How to Vote Cards, the shared billboards, letters of endorsement mailed out under your name, et cetera, all of which was by arrangement with the candidate concerned, did that give you pause as to whether you might either be seen to be or in fact be a group for the purpose of the Local Government Electoral Act?

W No. I think it's fair to say there was much discussion amongst councillors whether – I think it was the 2012 election, too, whether we nominate as a group. But there's fierce independence in our council, and it's probably the strength of the Moreton Bay Council and why they've survived so long relatively intact against the flow of councils in Queensland.

(Fiercely independent? What was that February vote again? Oh yes, 208 for, 5 against.)

CA So far as voting is concerned, at least, I think the effect of what you are saying is that, in your view, there are no groups for the purpose of voting on council business?

W That's correct.

CA We have mentioned disclosure previously. You know that personal disclosure returns of gifts have to be made to the Electoral Commission after the election, and you did so after the 2016 election; correct?

W Correct.

CA Your personal disclosure return, which we'll go to a bit later, shows large donations from Moreton Futures Trust; correct?

W Correct.

CA Was 2016 the first election campaign in which you'd received donations from Moreton Futures Trust?

W No, the second. 2012.

CA Okay. Who did you get this approach from, whether you would accept support from this Moreton Futures Trust?

W I think there would have been at least two councillors talking about it. I'm pretty sure it was Mike Charlton that approached me in the first instance. I had never had any involvement with the trust. I had always run my own show. So your spider senses are tingling, and I asked about the trust and I remember one of the people I asked was the longest-serving councillor, (Paul) Tully at that time, and Brian Battersby, who I have enormous respect for, and I said, "Do you know anything about this trust?", and he said that he did.

CA That is Brian Battersby?

W Yes, and that the people behind it were honourable, upstanding members of the Pine Rivers community. I'm not sure at that time whether it was Kirby Leeke or not, but I did take it on Brian's authority that - I said, "Is there anything to worry about?", and he said, "No, no, they're all really good people" and rattled off a couple of names.

CA All right. Did you subsequently meet or speak to anyone more directly connected with the trust –

W No.

CA No-one outside of council?

W No.

CA Before 2012

W No, I didn't even know who made up the organisation.

CA Having made some inquiry, by the sound of it, of Mr Battersby, did you agree that you would allow yourself to be the recipient of money from this trust?

W Yes.

CA And from what you tell us, you didn't have any discussion or direct contact with persons who might be trustees or involved in the administration of it?

W No, and – this is a long time ago, so you've got to rely on foggy memory.

(Better than winning the lottery. Moreton Futures Trust declared a donation of $110,500 to Allan

Sutherland for 2012 and supported no other councillor. And Cr Sutherland told the CCC, 'I didn't even know who made up the organisation.')

I remember talking to my wife about it, and she said – she's a very cautious lady – "Who's behind it?", and I just turned around and I said, "Well, I can only take it on Brian's and Mike's word that they sound like they're the old crowd." I remember saying to Gayle, "I think it's Bryan Galvin and all that business mob, whoever they are", but I said, "Brian Battersby and them say they're all really upstanding people."

CA Did you find out for the purpose of the 2012 election who the trustees were?

W No, I don't think I ever knew who the trustees were.

CA You did, in the end, receive money –

W Yes.

CA – for the 2012 campaign from Moreton Futures Trust?

W Correct.

CA And that created an obligation to report or disclose in your subsequent return?

W Yes, correct.

CA And you did make a disclosure of having received money from Moreton Futures Trust?

W Correct.

CA You really ought to have included the names of the trustees on your disclosure, Mr Sutherland, shouldn't you?

W I found out that this week.

(A colleague and I asked Cr Sutherland in 2015 who were the trustees of Moreton Futures Trust and what was his relationship with the trust and he replied all questions about the trust should be referred to it.

The CCC, on handing down its report, wrote of the omission of trustee details from two councillors' disclosure returns: 'The CCC examined disclosure returns and bank accounts for Crs Sutherland and Flannery and found that both councillors had recorded all of the gifts they had received from MFT (Moreton Futures Trust) in their returns.

'However, the details about MFT that the councillors recorded in their return did not comply with section 109 of the LGE Act. Specifically, the returns did not state the names and residential or business addresses of MFT's trustees as required. The CCC does not suggest that this omission was done dishonestly. At the public hearing, Cr Sutherland stated that he had only become aware of the requirement that week.'

My colleague and I asked Cr Sutherland about the trust and the trustees in late 2015. He either sought no advice about his obligations regarding the trust and the trustees or he received bad advice. We, on the other hand, received excellent advice from law Professor Henry Higgins.)

CA Do you understand now that the rules actually require, in the case of trusts, to identify the trustees or persons who are responsible for paying the money?

W Yes.
CA And you would accept, wouldn't you, that that is a transparency measure?
W There's –
CA Because otherwise who is really to know who is behind such a trust and who is in fact funding you?
W I understand that and I think there has been a lot of – how would you say it? – editorial on members of that trust over many years.

(I would suggest editorial on members of MTF would be pretty close to zip, rather than lots. Walter Burns and I tried in vain.)

CA You've already mentioned a couple of names. Dr Ryan?
W Yes.
CA How do you know him?
W Until probably – what month are we in now? Until probably 15 or 16 months ago, I never knew him. I'd never met him, that I can recall, at all. I had a particularly difficult health situation both before and during the election.
CA You consulted him for health reasons, did you?
W Well, he was recommended to me because –
CA I don't want to know about your health. That's private.
W He was recommended to me because we couldn't find out what was going on, and I knew there was something wrong. It was Mike Charlton that said, "You should go and see Dr John." It was probably the best move I ever made.
CA So he became your physician?

W Yes.

CA Do you know Kirby Leeke?

W I had never met him in my life until Brian Battersby's send-off.

CA That was approximately when?

W I think it was January or it may have been February 2016.

CA He (Brian Battersby) retired, I guess, did he?

W Yes, he did.

CA He didn't seek re-election?

W No, no.

CA Is that the first time you met him?

W Yes. He come up to me and said "Mayor" and shook my hand, and I said – well, there was a lot of people there. It was a big send-off. I said, "How are you going?" He said, "You don't know me, do you?" words to that effect, and I said, "No", and he said, "My name's Kirby Leeke", and I said, "Moreton Futures Trust?", and he said, "Yes." That was at the send-off.

CA Moreton Futures Trust did substantially fund your 2016 campaign?

W Correct.

CA What I'm really suggesting is that, at some point, you must have been made aware by some means that there was going to be money coming in?

W We did speak –

CA And it wasn't a trifle?

W It was over the phone.

CA With Kirby?

W Once the establishment was made that they'd be working, he said, "Who should I contact?", or, "Who can we go to with your campaign?", and I said, "My wife. I keep away from that sort of thing as much as possible", and the bridge was made between Kirby – very early on in January or February, whichever time it was, I'm not quite sure of, between my wife and Kirby and any subsequent conversations to that were almost solely with Gayle and Kirby.
CA What was her role in your campaigning?
W Made sure the bills were getting paid and done the terrible job of booth roster. She takes a month off work every election to work out the logistics.
CA Was there any mention, in any conversation that you had with Kirby Leeke, about what kind of money they might be able to make available to you?
W No, no.
CA You didn't know that?
W No, I didn't know how much. I knew how much I needed for a campaign.
CA Yes.
W That's the job of the campaign committee, is to go out and, for want of a better word, rattle the can.
CA But you must have been aware that the amounts that were being reimbursed on the invoices were substantial, amounting, in the end, to over $100,000?
W Yes.
CA Were you aware of that, though? That you were if not the sole, certainly the central participant, of all

the money that was raised in the Moreton Futures Trust?

W Well, I would have hoped that I was the only mayoral candidate that they were supporting, yes.

CA You mentioned a name David Trask. You know him; he is a friend of yours?

W He's a really good mate.

CA A good mate, yes. Is he on your campaign committee?

W No, but he turned up to a couple of meetings. He's not – he's not part of the central heart of the meeting, the committee.

CA Do you know of any involvement by him in raising donations for the Moreton Futures Trust?

W Certainly. He's probably the best there is.

CA Well, I think when you were being asked about this in your interview before, you said words to the effect that David Trask may have been rattling the can around the business community. Is that correct?

W I just said he is probably the best there is. I wouldn't like to be in a room with David when he's chasing money.

(Musical interlude with a can-rattling solo: *Rattle the can*. 'I'm the best that's ever bin.' *Rattle the can*.)

CA I've just shown you the Moreton Futures Trust return for the 2016 election. Have you seen that before?

W Yes.

CA When did you first look at it?

W During the course of the investigation.

CA Recent months?

W Yes.

CA Did you make a point of looking at it, or not, after the election, after it was lodged?

W After the election, no, I didn't, and I didn't really care. After the election, I was more intent on trying to get myself into some sort of shape that I didn't have to resign. I wasn't real flash. It was probably the last thing on my mind at that stage after the election.

CA You say, I think, that you didn't want to know the contents of the return, or weren't interested?

W It's hard to have a conflict when you don't know who's there. But if you do know who's there, you've got a conflict. Do you walk or don't you walk? It presents one of the issues.

CA Would you accept that anyone who chose to make the comparison between this third party return of Moreton Futures Trust and your personal declaration of having received money from Moreton Futures Trust would reveal that the use of an intermediary, being the trust, does not conceal that you benefited heavily from developer donations to your campaign?

W If you're going to be interested enough to look at that – they're all online. It's not hard. You look at one. Who is Moreton Futures Trust? Then look up Moreton Futures Trust and see what they are. That's what's happening in the community as we speak.

14

IT WAS PROBABLY A CO-INCIDENCE that two women – Christine Monsour and Lyn Devereaux – were the renegades in their respective councils of Pine Rivers and Caboolture. Women were poorly represented in Pine Rivers and Caboolture councils and women are now under-represented in Moreton Bay Regional Council. Women are so under-represented in all councils, it is difficult to make a comparative case things would be different, and better, if there were more of them. But as meeting statistics of Moreton Bay Regional Council show, Councillors Brooke Savige and Denise Sims have on occasion spoken and voted against the groupthink. Both women are politically conservative but the two first-termers have raised their hands to offer alternative voices in council.

Rumour has it both women have been carpeted for not being team players in a council described by Mayor Sutherland as being fiercely independent.

As author Thomas Keneally explored in his novel *The Chant of Jimmy Blacksmith*, rumour can sometimes be the only media for suppressed news. Another Keneally novel is *Gossip from the Forest*. Where there are compliant media and intimidated, legally bound public servants, rumour can be a carriage of information. The shortcomings of rumour are a lack of nuance and the distortion of Chinese whispers. Still in the lingo of the make-do Australian, it's 'better than nothing'.

Rumour has it a couple of 'the boys' on Pine Rivers Shire Council persuaded Yvonne Chapman to run for the job of first Mayor in 1994. The Local Government Act of 1993 enlarged the responsibilities and law-making powers of councils to do such things as infrastructure and development planning and approval, provision of community services, and environmental protection. With the added responsibilities, being a councillor became a full-time job. Preferential voting replaced first-past-the-post. Two governance measures were open council meetings and a detailed interests register. The position of shire chairman was replaced with mayor. The following year 1994 was the first election to ring in the changes.

The word was two of the boys wanted former National Party State Cabinet Minister Yvonne Chapman to run for mayor and one of the boys would dethrone her at a subsequent election. That was the A-plan.

No one ran for councillor or mayor on a party ticket in 1994 but it was obvious the mayoral race would be a showdown between Mrs Chapman and Liberal Party member Rob Akers. This was well before the Liberals and Nationals merged in 2008 to form the LNP. The two conservative parties did have a long history of sometimes strained coalition government in Queensland before that coalition was turfed out of state office in 1989.

Despite her history of standing as a Liberal for an earlier Pine Rivers Shire Council, Mrs Chapman was a rock-solid member and supporter of the National Party and its predecessor the Country Party. She would have relished the opportunity to go up against the Liberal Rob Akers. National Party members detested the Labor Party politicians almost as much as they hated the Liberals. Politicians having greater animosity to their allies than to their opponents is nothing new. German sociologist Georg Simmel was commenting on it 120 years ago.

Rob Akers easily outpolled Mrs Chapman 16,652 votes to 13,894. But Mrs Chapman prevailed on preferences.

Optional preferential voting replaced the compulsory version and was in place in 2016. Exchange of preferences among candidates was rare. I suggested to one candidate he would profit from a preference exchange which had been offered to him. He replied he had been advised not to do such a deal. As it turned out he ran second and would almost certainly have been elected if he had done the preference swap.

In April 2016, Labor pulled a swiftie, without notice tacking on to an LNP bill an amendment to return to full preferential voting. The two politicians from the minnow Katter Party supported it as it makes their preferences count for more in other seats. In the full preferential system, a valid vote has every square marked and the votes for each eliminated candidate are transferred down to the next selected candidate. Every valid vote eventually goes to either of the last two candidates standing.

At the State and Federal level, full preferential voting favours Labor as the preferences of the Greens who poll on average about 10 per cent of the vote (less in Queensland) flow at a predictable rate to Labor. The preferences of voters for populist protest parties such as One Nation are less predictable.

At council elections, without parties but with full preferential voting, protest votes will flow away from incumbent councillors. If there are changes in councils at the 2020 council elections, let's hope more women are elected.

At the 2016 Moreton Bay Council election, 13 councillors were elected and four were women. Two of those elected – Cr Savige and Cr Sims were newbies – so in the 2012 Council, two out of 13 councillors (15.38 per cent) were women.

In Ipswich, in 2016, four out of 11 elected councillors were women and at the Gold Coast, six of 15 elected candidates were women.

Brisbane City Council runs parties at elections. You might hope that parties promote gender equity but only nine of the 26 candidates elected in 2016 were women. I support quotas to work towards 50 per cent pre-selection of women. I have little sympathy for that cliché of selecting on talent rather than gender. Given our present gender skew, how did it come to pass that men became much more talented for politics than women? Positive discrimination to redress bigotry is a good thing in my book.

What's the number one reason there are fewer women elected to councils? In independent councils, they do not run and in party-dominated councils, they do not get pre-selected in winnable wards. At the Moreton Bay election of 2016, 46 candidates stood for divisions or mayor and 11 of these were women. At a simple statistical level, women did well to take four seats out of 13. In other words electors will vote for women at council elections.

I have spoken to academics and candidates over the years on why women do not stand as candidates. Suggested reasons, which are not convincing, are women not wanting to play in the boys' club and too many other commitments. Women do take on the boys on community issues and they dominate many outside-home community groups such as P and Cs. A commitment to State or Federal Parliament would seem a greater challenge on a woman's time than serving on a local council.

I believe the two reasons women do not nominate for council are they have less money than men and the boys' club anoints its successors.

15

ALTHOUGH ALLAN SUTHERLAND did not meet Dr John Ryan until early 2016, the anti-fluoride general practitioner has been lobbying councils over many years.

From the early 2000s in Australia, the coalition against fluoridation of the water supply had been lobbying Australian Governments. It seems proponents of natural remedies have joined some GPs in the crusade.

Moreton Futures Trustee Dr John Ryan was Chairman of Professionals Against Water Fluoridation (PAWF) which claimed to represent 'some 3000 doctors, dentists, scientists and other health professionals in Australia, with significant concerns concerning the Safety and Efficacy of Water Fluoridation.

'Water fluoridation supporters seek to relegate those opposed to their views as "nutters", including me – a medical practitioner vitally interested in early intervention medicine,' Dr Ryan said.

In 2004, when John Ryan was a member of Friends of Pine Rivers, Dr Ryan and PAWF wrote an open letter to Queensland councillors and state parliamentarians. At the time, neither Brisbane nor Pine Rivers councils fluoridated their water supplies.

The letter said PAWF had grave concerns about proposals to introduce fluoridation.

In February 2008, Dr Ryan made a presentation against fluoridation of the water supply.to Queensland Premier Anna Bligh. The pitch was unsuccessful and later that year the State Government passed a law that all Queensland drinking water would be treated with fluoride.

In 2012, the LNP government, headed by one-term Premier Campbell Newman, passed legislation allowing individual councils to decide whether to have fluoride, reversing the previous Bligh government mandate.

In 2013, retired New York chemistry teacher and co-founder of the Fluoride Action Network, Dr Paul Connett, visited Australia on his crusade supported by Australian Fluoride Action of which Dr Ryan is a prominent member. Dr Connett who has a PhD in chemistry addressed Moreton Bay Regional Councillors on February 13, 2013.

Cr James Houghton, a cousin of Allan Sutherland, said Dr Connett convinced him fluoride was a poison which should be removed from the council water supply. Cr Houghton said he had received other convincing information from the public, a 'naturalist' medical practitioner he did not name, and the internet. Cr Sutherland said he was not making a commitment but Council would investigate the process of removing fluoride.

On February 23, Cr Sutherland told ABC Television 7.30 reporter Matt Wordsworth, 'I think it's fair to say most councillors would be in favour of taking fluoride out of the water supply if the opportunity arose and if it could be done cost effectively.'

Mr Wordsworth and I worked together at the *Queensland Times* in Ipswich so Matt might feel nostalgic if he covers the continuing saga of former Mayor Paul Pisasale.

Mr Wordsworth also questioned Cr Houghton who concluded with, 'I've adopted an old adage, when in doubt anyway, leave out. When in doubt, leave out.'

'When in doubt, leave it out' is an old adage from journalism which I have not heard in any other context. 'When it doubt, take it out' is an old adage from surgical medicine but I am sure contemporary surgeons would not support such a cavalier approach. The World Health Organization (WHO) leads a group of more than 150 major world-wide health organisations in favour of water fluoridation. Public Health England, the Australian Medical Association (AMA) and the Australian Dental Association (ADA) support water fluoridation.

WHO and the University of Sheffield, UK, issued a 2004 paper with their position on fluoridation. 'Water fluoridation, where technically feasible and culturally acceptable, has substantial advantages in public health; alternatively, fluoridation of salt and milk fluoridation schemes may be considered for prevention of dental caries.'

New South Wales began fluoridation of the water supply in 1956. I recall a scientist telling me how she and her family moved to Brisbane in the late 1970s. She was 12 and her youngest brother was 6. By the time she was in her mid 20s she had good teeth and her teenage brother had bad teeth. She put it down to six more years of fluoridated water.

Almost 200 million Americans are supplied with artificially fluoridated water. In addition to the US and England, countries with high rates of fluoridated water include Spain and the Republic of Ireland, Australia, Brazil, Chile, Malaysia, and Singapore.

The US, Canada and Ireland have reduced the level of fluoridation from 1ppm to .7ppm, but there are no plans for abolition in those countries. Ppm stands for parts per million.

Ultimately, it was decided removing fluoride from Moreton Bay Region water supply was too hard.

'It would be difficult for any council in south-east Queensland to stop fluoridation given our communities are connected by the one water-supply network,' Cr Sutherland said.

It was possible for Moreton Bay Council to go it alone as Seqwater pointed out, 'If only some local governments decided that the supply of fluoridated water . . . should cease . . . the obligation would lie with those local governments intending to discontinue fluoridation to implement this decision by negotiation with Seqwater.'

While Moreton Bay Region did not remove fluoride, other Queensland councils, mainly rural, removed the fluoride from their water supplies. Such decisions have prompted calls for the State Labor Government to re-impose the mandate of fluoridation. But this will not happen with an election waiting in the wings.

Since 2012, nineteen local governments in Queensland have switched off fluoride plants:

Local Government Area	Year switched off
Aurukun Shire Council	2015
Cairns	2013
Cherbourg	2012
Doomadgee	2012
Douglas (when part of Cairns)	2013
Fraser Coast	2013
Gladstone	2016
Hinchinbrook	2017
Livingstone (when part of Rockhampton)	2013
Longreach	2014
Mackay	2016
North Burnett	2013
Northern Peninsula Area (Bamaga)	2012
Palm Island	2012
Rockhampton	2013
South Burnett	2013
Southern Downs	2015
Torres	2012
Yarrabah	2012

There is no evidence and I do not believe that Dr John Ryan used his associations with Friends of Pine Rivers and Moreton Futures Trust to reward council candidates sceptical of fluoridation of the water supply.

But he was evasive in 2004 when a colleague on the Pine Rivers Press sought explanation about the membership and aims of Friends of Pine Rivers. He conceded to the CCC hearings he refused to answer my questions on his trusteeship of the Moreton Futures Trust. Fellow trustee Kirby Leeke did not put Dr Ryan's name on his initial third party disclosure form for 2012.

It was only after persistent inquiries from me to the Electoral Commission of Queensland that Mr Leeke was advised to revise his disclosure and he included Dr Ryan as trustee. I have not seen anywhere the disclosure of Dr Ryan's transfer of more than $20,000 from Friends of Pine Rivers to Moreton Futures Trust.

Is such opaqueness about third-party donors worth the trouble of continuing a system of third parties? I would say no. If we do keep third parties, their genesis, ideals, associations, and membership need to be fully disclosed.

16

DURING THE EVIDENCE of Allan Sutherland, we learned how he kept at arm's length from fundraising for his campaign, and its major vehicle Moreton Futures Trust. Another witness, Trent Dixon, offered evidence pertinent to these claims.

Mr Dixon worked on marketing for Cr Sutherland's campaigns of 2012 and 2016. He was paid for his work on each campaign.

I filed a report on Mr Dixon's appearance before the hearing:

THE CCC inquiry into the 2016 Moreton Bay Regional Council election yesterday heard mayoral candidate Allan Sutherland discussed soliciting a $20,000 donation from developer Robert Comiskey.

Former Redcliffe Leagues Club marketing manager Trent Dixon was a witness at the hearing in Fortitude Valley into the 2016 council elections of Moreton Bay, the Gold Coast, and Ipswich.

The presiding officer at the inquiry is Alan MacSporran and Glen Rice is Counsel Assisting.

Mr Dixon spoke of campaign meetings at Allan Sutherland's home leading up to the 2016 election. 'Directly before the election they (the meetings) were weekly.'

Mr Rice asked Mr Dixon who were at these meetings.

'Well, the Mayor and his wife. His daughter, Emma. Noel Powell. Myself. (Councillor) James Houghton. (Cr) Mike Charlton. Probably not as regularly for those two. Corinne,' Mr Dixon said.

He said the meetings were mainly about strategy and campaign talking points such as the proposed Petrie University and the Redcliffe rail and technical issues, including the wording on joint how-to-vote cards.

Fundraising was also discussed though to a lesser extent. 'When that election came around in 2016 and they were fundraising for it, I went to (developer) Rob (Comiskey) and said, 'Is that something you're interested in?'" Mr Dixon said.

Counsel Assisting, Mr Rice, asked, 'Did the Mayor, for example, raise his name (Robert Comiskey) and suggest that you speak with him about it?'

'He may have or it might have been me suggesting it,' Mr Dixon said.

He agreed Allan Sutherland and he had a discussion on Mr Comiskey donating.

'Was a figure mentioned?' Mr Rice asked.

'The figure that Rob paid ($20,000),' Mr Dixon said.

Allan Sutherland told Mr Dixon to ask Mr Comiskey to make out the cheque to Moreton Futures Trust, Mr Dixon said.

He gave the cheque to Cr Sutherland at a place 'like a sports centre' on Bracken Ridge Rd.

Transcript #9
Abridged by Bernie Dowling

Witness Trent Dixon, June 13, 2017
PO, Presiding Officer Alan MacSporran QC
CA, Counsel Assisting, Glen Rice QC
W, Trent Dixon

PO Good morning, everyone. This is a hearing of the Crime and Corruption Commission conducted under section 176 of the Crime and Corruption Act 2001.

Do not disrupt or interrupt the hearing. Switch your mobile phones off or to silent or any electronic devices you have to silent and refrain from moving around the room while the hearing is in session. Everyone should also be aware that we are live streaming the recording of the public hearing today.

The Commission resolved recently, as you are aware, to extend the public hearings to include the Logan Council, and that is the prime purpose of the hearings over the next few days, although there are some tidy-up brackets of evidence relating to at least the Moreton Shire Council to be led in this bracket.

(It is Moreton Bay Regional Council but Mr MacSporran is using the more familiar concept of a shire as an area of local government.)

I am conducting the hearing as the Presiding Officer, and Mr Glen Rice QC has been appointed as Counsel Assisting the inquiry. Pursuant to sections 5 and 5C of the Recording of Evidence Act 1962, I direct that any evidence to be given and any ruling, direction or other matter be recorded by recording equipment.

At the original hearing, I did make a direction under subsection 197 (5) of the Crime and Corruption Act 2001 in relation to the evidence to be given here by witnesses. For those of you who are not familiar with that, I will make the direction again, so it's clear.

Witnesses who come here are not entitled to refuse to answer questions. It is a compulsory hearing process, but there are protections given in the Act if I make this direction so that people can be assured that whatever they say here, even if it tends to incriminate them, will not be able to be used against them in any subsequent proceedings. So it is a standard protection. It is what's called a blanket protection that I am proposing to give the witnesses.

(The protection of witnesses does not extend to allowing perjury, which can be prosecuted in court.)

I direct for the purpose of these proceedings that all answers given by an individual and all documents or things produced by an individual are to be regarded as having been given or produced on objection by the individual. That simply means that every witness now has the protection of the Act, and whatever they say, as I say, even if incriminating, cannot be used against them in subsequent proceedings.

Mr Rice, are you ready to proceed or do you need more time?

CA   No, Commissioner. There are six witnesses whose attendance is scheduled today. The first of those, I call Trent Alan Dixon.
PO   Thank you.
CA   Is your name Trent Alan Dixon?
W   Yes.
CA   Mr Dixon , you have some tertiary qualifications in marketing, I think?
W   Yes.
CA   What are they?
W   Bachelor of Commerce in marketing and a Masters of Marketing Management.
CA   You worked for a time, I think, as marketing manager at the Redcliffe Leagues Club?
W   Yes.
CA   Over what time frame, Mr Dixon?
W   About six years, just short.
CA   What years, do you remember?
W   I started in December 2005.
CA   Do you know some of the councillors at the Moreton Bay Regional Council?
W   Yes.
CA   I will just give you a few names. Do you know the Mayor, Allan Sutherland?
W   Yes.
CA   Councillor Mike Charlton?
W   Yes.
CA   Councillor James Houghton?
W   Yes.
CA   To take Councillor Sutherland first, how did you first come to know him?

W I met him through my time at the leagues club. When I first started, it was Christmas time. I met him at a Christmas function. That was the first time I met him, December 2005.

CA Did you have some ongoing contact with him subsequent to that?

W Yes.

CA In what capacity?

W Mainly at various functions, but the club expanded during my time there with different developments – pools and shopping centres and whatnot – so the politicians were often there to open things, cut ribbons, that sort of stuff, so it was ongoing.

CA Was it a professional relationship or did you become friends?

W Professional.

CA Councillor Sutherland was a candidate for Mayor in the 2012 election; correct?

W Yes.

CA Did you offer some assistance with his 2012 election campaign?

W Yes.

CA What was that?

W Marketing advice.

CA How did that come about?

W He asked me.

CA Well, what was the content of what you did for him during that campaign?

W I gave him general marketing advice or principles on the marketing collateral he was developing for his campaign.
CA Was there a fee attached to the service you gave?
W Yes.
CA So did you charge him for it?
W Yes.
CA And you were paid for that?
W Yes.
CA Do you recall what amount?
W No.
CA Some thousands?
W Probably, yes. Yes.
CA We will move forward to the 2016 campaign where Mr Sutherland was also the successful candidate for Mayor in that election. Did you play some role in his campaign?
W Yes, similar. A similar role.
CA Can you give us some detail of what you did?
W The same as the previous one. I gave him advice on his marketing collateral, making sure he had the right message via the right marketing channel to the right people.
CA What do you mean by "marketing collateral"?
W Well, his campaign went across a number of different mediums, from billboards to flyers to newspaper. I gave him basic advice on how to make sure the content was engaging and effective and, whatever the message was, we were using the right medium for the target audience. Just basic marketing principles, really.

CA Did you attend some meetings for campaign purposes?
W Yes.
CA Were they held at a particular location?
W At his house.
CA With what regularity?
W Directly before the election they were weekly, but they probably started off every few weeks and became more regular the closer we got to the election.
CA Were you then a regular attendee?
W Yes.
CA Did you go to all of them, so far as you know?
W I think so, as far as I know.
CA Were there other regular attendees at these meetings?
W Yes.
CA Can you remember who they were?
W Yes, most of them, yes.
CA Can you give us some names?
W Well, the Mayor and his wife. His daughter, Emma. Noel Powell. Myself. James Houghton. Mike Charlton. Probably not as regularly for those two. Corinne. And there was another gentleman. I just don't recall his name.
CA You mentioned Noel Powell. What was his capacity within these meetings?
W I guess it was similar to mine, in that he just gave his advice, but he's sort more of a – although they were informal meetings, he might have been

considered more of a chairperson to keep the meeting going, moving on to different topics.

CA Was there a degree of formality about it, in the sense were there minutes kept?

W There might have been minutes kept, yes. I think there was – not formal minutes that were distributed to all of the attendees each week, but I'm sure Gayle or Emma was probably taking notes, yes.

CA You mentioned the other councillors, Mr Charlton and Mr Houghton, not as regular in attendance as you?

W They were pretty regular, but sometimes they couldn't stay for the whole time. Yes, they were there, but they might miss one here or there.

CA Can you give us your recollection as to the content of the meetings?

W A number of different things. Key points that the Mayor was pushing to get re-elected, like university, the rail and free Wi-Fi, some key points to his platform were discussed and how best to communicate that to the different audiences. There were updates on fundraising and expenditures of the marketing campaign, and that was probably it.

CA Did meetings include the subject of fundraising?

W Briefly.

CA Was there any discussion about joint How to Vote Cards?

W Yes.

CA Do you remember any of the detail of that?

W Not really, just that they talked about it.

CA Was there any discussion about other collateral, such as signage?

W All collateral, all marketing collateral – billboards, radio ads, everything was discussed at the meetings.

CA Did those discussions include Councillors Charlton and Houghton?

W Yes.

CA Was there any discussion about payment of expenses for such signage and other collateral?

W There was. Not a lot. Just sort of an update from time to time how much the different campaigns were going to cost and whether we could go ahead with them or whether we have to reduce, you know, the size of it, if it was a flyer drop, for instance. Just general updates on that from time to time.

CA Do you know of Moreton Futures Trust?

W Yes.

CA How did you first hear about it, do you remember?

W During the campaign, I heard about it.

CA The 2016 election campaign?

W Yes.

CA How did you come to hear about it?

W Well, a person called Rob Comiskey was donating to the campaign and he wanted to know who to make the cheque out to. At that stage, I didn't know so I found out – I raised it and asked and that's who I had to make it out to – or Rob had to make it out to.

CA Did you have some communication with him about that?

W With Rob, yes.
CA Was that in person or over the phone?
W Person, I think. In person.
CA How did that originate, do you remember?
W I don't remember how it originated.
CA What led you to do that? Why did you approach him?
W Because they were fundraising for the campaign.
CA How did his name crop up?
W I don't recall.
CA Well, something must have led you to seek him out, as you apparently did?
W Well, I know him. I know him well and I know, from years back, he was trying to improve relationships with the government, so –
CA Were you asked by anyone to approach him and see if he would be interested?
W The Mayor – he might have asked me or I might have suggested it. I don't recall.
CA Did the Mayor, for example, raise his name and suggest that you speak with him about it?
W Well, that's what I'm saying. He may have or it might have been me suggesting it.
CA In any event, you had some discussion with him on the subject of donating?
W Yes.
CA Was a figure mentioned?
W Yes.
CA What figure of potential donation was mentioned?
W The figure that Rob paid.

CA I think it was $20,000?

W Yes, correct.

CA Is that the amount that was referred to in your discussion?

W Yes.

CA Well, how did it advance from there in terms of Moreton Futures Trust?

W Well, Rob agreed to give the money. At that stage, I hadn't heard of the Moreton Futures Trust. Then when Rob asked, you know, "How does it work and who do I give the money to?" I then went and asked.

CA Asked who?

W The Mayor, and he said, "To the Moreton Bay (sic) Futures Trust", so I gave –

CA Was that the first you had heard of it?

W Yes.

CA At that time?

W Yes.

CA What did he explain in terms of how the payment should be made?

W Nothing really, other than make the cheque to Moreton Bay Futures Trust. He didn't really delve into what the trust was, how it worked or anything like that.

CA So you got this information from the Mayor that it should be made to Moreton Futures Trust?

W Yes.

CA Did you go back to Mr Comiskey with that information?

W Yes.

CA Did he query that as to, "Why do it this way?"

W Yes, he did. He just wanted to make sure, you know, that that money was going to help the Mayor's campaign and probably a couple of other councillors that he endorsed or liked, or whatever, and so he had some questions about that, but –
CA What were you able to tell him?
W Not much.
CA Well, did you satisfy his query?
W Well, I must have, because he paid it. He paid the cheque to Moreton Bay Futures Trust.
CA You must have had some information to give him because he asked you about it
W Basically, what I just said. I told him it's a trust fund. I think I said that, you know, all the councillors can access it, but it's going to help the Mayor's fund, and probably all the funds in it will be exhausted by the election is over and there's probably not going to be much change.
CA Where did you get that information from to be able to pass it on to him?
W From the Mayor.
CA So you did ask the Mayor about the operation of the Moreton Futures Trust?
W No, not the operation of it.
CA I see.
W Oh, well, possibly. He was reasonably vague in his explanation, like I said, so I just told Rob what I got told, which wasn't much, and moved on.
CA You passed that on to Mr Comiskey?
W Yes.
CA He was happy with what you told him?

W Yes.
CA Did he proceed to make the donation?
W Yes.
CA In what form? Was it a cheque?
W Yes.
CA What happened to the cheque? Did you receive it?
W Yes.
CA What did you do with it?
W I gave it to the Mayor.
CA Do you recall the occasion on which you did that?
W I don't know the date.
CA But where and how?
W I was driving back after I collected it from the Comiskey office and met the Mayor on Bracken Ridge Road at a – it's like a sports centre. I pulled over there and gave it to him.

17

ALLAN SUTHERLAND LIKES to promote himself as always having been a resolute supporter of the Redcliffe rail line. That is not quite right.

Redcliffe City Council with Cr Sutherland as Mayor did support the proposed Petrie to Kippa-Ring rail line but his resolve waivered in 2008. The State Government under Premier Anna Bligh wanted a busway first with the rail line put on the backburner until the late 2020s. The proposed transport corridor was to include a dedicated busway from Petrie to Mango Hill and bus lanes to Redcliffe. Cr Sutherland, new Mayor of Moreton Bay Region, agreed to the plan.

Wise heads in the community figured authorities had been promising a railway for 100 years. Rail supporters were not holding out for a promise of one in twenty years from 2008. They figured if a new busway was built that would be the end of the railway. A new residents' group Rail '09 joined the established Where's Our Railway? to persuade Premier Anna Bligh to change her mind and to prioritise the rail.

I had been reporting on the efforts of Where's Our Railway? and other rail supporters over the years and continued to do stories on them and the new group, Rail '09.

A State Election loomed in 2009 and the seats of Kallangur, Murrumba, and Redcliffe were near the proposed railway line which would bring employment and transport to jobs. Studies have shown that unemployed people without private transport have better prospects of finding work if they live close to a railway station. Electric trains and noise barriers mitigate against the aural unpleasantness of living near rail. Residents of other seats such as Pine Rivers and Morayfield might respond positively to a promise of a new line. The campaigns of Rail '09 and Where's Our Railway? made sense and, in 2009, Premier Bligh gave an election promise of a Redcliffe rail line. The opposition, the newly formed LNP, matched it and Allan Sutherland jumped back on the train. Anna Bligh and Labor won the 2009 election.

Luckily for the born-again rail lovers, 2010 was a Federal election year and Labor Member for Petrie, Yvette D'Ath, persuaded Federal Transport and Infrastructure Minister Anthony Albanese there were votes in the line. The Julia Gillard Labor government duly limped over the electoral line. Ms D'Ath retained her seat, only to lose Petrie in 2013, but gain the State seat of Redcliffe in a 2014 by-election. She became Queensland Attorney-General.

Where's Our Railway? and Rail '09 received little credit for the railway. I was sidelined from reporting on the railway as my editors patted themselves on the back for their parts in securing the line. I don't know if anyone from Where's Our Railway? or Rail

'09 was invited to join Prime Minister Malcolm Turnbull and Mayor Allan Sutherland on the first train. Cr Sutherland wore a quaint suit with the jacket opened to reveal a floral waistcoat complementing the white beard and moustache which he has sported since his mystery illness. He looked, for all the world, like a 19th century American railway baron. I guess that was the idea. My invitation to ride that first train got lost in the mail.

Previously, I was invited to travel on the first electric tilt-train from Brisbane to Rockhampton. I sat right up front, beside the driver who explained to me how sensors in the tracks controlled the train's speed. Although cut from the history of Redcliffe rail, I retain fond memory of the tilt-train maiden voyage. Oh, and I am footnote number 14 in the Wikipedia entry for 'Redcliffe Peninsula railway line'.

Residents groups such as Where's Our Railway? and Rail '09 make positive contributions to our community. Councils and councillors are suspicious of them. Council rewards its many community volunteers with a morning tea each year but among the scone munchers are volunteers equally committed to monitoring council governance. Cr Sutherland is also interested in governance as he is chair of the Moreton Bay Regional Council governance committee. The ethics training he was obliged to take in 2013 must have paid off.

Residents' groups challenge the authority of council, and powerbrokers within the local government do not like that. Worse the dissident groups might encourage one or more of their members to stand for council. Councils better get used to residents' action groups because only death or relocation will stop the righteous anger of baby boomers at perceived official wrongdoing.

Ethics training in 2013 was the wilted-lettuce beating Cr Sutherland took after he was referred to the Crime and Misconduct Commission (CMC). He and developer 'good mate' David Trask concocted a political strategy against mayoral opponent Chris Whiting before the 2012 election.

Cr Whiting first became Cr Sutherland's bitter enemy when the former questioned whether Moreton Bay Council was taking too much profit as a shareholder of the water distributor, Unitywater. The implication was ratepayers could be paying less for water.

In the lead-up to the 2012 election, a Trask company gave $1000 towards Mr Whiting's campaign. Cr Sutherland watched the still Cr Whiting's interests register and the Trojan donation failed to appear.

Council CEO John Rauber reported Cr Whiting to the CMC but the case was dismissed. By 2017, Mr Whiting was State Member for Murrumba and planning to contest the seat of Bancroft on November 25, after a redistribution. His previous council division as well as Murrumba and Bancroft contained or contain Mr Whiting's heartland, the working class seaside suburb of Deception Bay.

Before the dismissal of the allegations against Cr Whiting, a local newspaper gleefully reported his unhappy oversight which resulted in his being caught in the Sutherland/ Trask 'trap'. I was working in the same office as that sister paper but was not asked my opinion on the story. I think I would have uncovered the Sutherland/Trask ruse but that would not have fitted the prevailing narrative of the newspaper which printed the story.

Cr Sutherland's underhand tactics were exposed when one of his colleagues secretly but legally recorded Cr Sutherland's boasting of the success of his 'trap'.

In 2013, the State Department of Local Government referred Cr Sutherland to the CMC which most surprisingly threw out the referral the same day for lack of jurisdiction.

The CMC said if any political detriment to Mr Whiting resulted from the alleged conduct of Cr Sutherland, that detriment would not trigger criminal offence provisions under the Local Government Act or the Queensland Criminal Code. Also the complaint against then Cr Chris Whiting by Moreton Bay CEO John Rauber did not contain false or misleading information and was not a vexatious complaint, in terms of the offence provisions in the Crime and Misconduct Act 2001. The alleged incident was referred to the Local Government Association Queensland

LGAQ CEO Greg Hallam acknowledged people would be offended by the revelations. He said it was unfortunate they made page one of the State newspaper. Mr Hallam said it was just a story about the rough and tumble of politics and Cr Sutherland had committed no criminal offence, nor breached any local government act.

Mr Hallam said Cr Sutherland would not be removed from his role on the policy committee of the LGAQ. Cr Sutherland would be asked to undergo ethics training, though.

18

MAYOR ALLAN SUTHERLAND and developer David Trask are two former Redcliffe tradies who made good. Redcliffe was a seaside city which lost its civic status in the amalgamation with Pine Rivers and Caboolture shires to form Moreton Bay Region. Redcliffe born and bred Allan Sutherland was an electrician and fellow Redcliffe lad David Trask was a marine motor mechanic. Former Moreton Bay Council CEO John Rauber had been a plumber and Cr Sutherland used to joke with me that Mr Rauber's former trade involved him regularly having his hand down a toilet. Who knew there was snobbery in trades?

Redcliffe residents are still bitter about the amalgamation. Caboolture and Pine Rivers denizens are rancorous too but nowhere near as hostile as the seaside people.

In 2008, I made fun of the amalgamation in my weekly humour column. 'Queensland Premier Beattie and three other people want the merger of the three local government areas so it is certain to go ahead,' I wrote.

Historically, state and local governments have had fights in Queensland so reducing potential combatants from three to one probably seemed like a good idea at the time to the State Government.

Allan Sutherland was Mayor of Redcliffe and campaigned against amalgamation. In one memorable stunt he pushed a wheelbarrow full of anti-amalgamation petitions from Redcliffe 35 or so kilometres to state Parliament House.

When he became Mayor of Moreton Bay, Cr Sutherland said unscrambling the egg to de-amalgamate was impossible. Whenever you hear the phrase 'unscrambling the egg' from a politician it means we could do something but we won't. Federal opposition leader Bill Shorten used the phrase recently when asked would Labor fix Australia's disastrous 'fibre to the node' internet broadband with fibre to the premises. Mr Shorten began his answer with 'we cannot unscramble the egg' and you knew the answer was no.

Another fierce opponent of amalgamation was Pine Rivers Shire Councillor Mike Charlton, now Deputy Mayor of Moreton Bay Region. Cr Charlton never uses the d-word, de-amalgamation.

For most of the past 25 years, the development business, Trask Corporation, was a partnership between Bob Trask and his younger brother David. Bob recently stepped aside from the organisation. I cannot remember which of the Trask brothers I interviewed after they gave $100,000 to Allan Sutherland's 2008 campaign to be the first Mayor of Moreton Region. I am unable to locate a copy of the article but I do remember the Trask bro' said Cr Sutherland, as Redcliffe Mayor, had reduced red tape. The developer felt Cr Sutherland would do an equally good job for the amalgamated region.

The remaining Trask bro' heads 40 companies involved in the development industry.

Transcript #10
Abridged by Bernie Dowling

Witness David Trask, June 13, 2017
PO, Presiding Officer Alan MacSporran QC
CA, Counsel Assisting, Glen Rice QC
W, David Trask

CA Is your name David Trask?
W Yes.
CA Mr Trask, you are a property developer by occupation; is that right?
W That's correct.
CA You operate through a range of corporations; is that so?
W Yes.
CA Trask Development Corporation being one of them?
W Mmm-hmm.
CA But there are a lot, aren't there?
W Yes.
CA Approximately how many, Mr Trask?
W Forty.
CA How long have you been in the property development business?

W Including my period as a salesperson, since 1989, I think it is.
CA And developing property in your own right?
W '94 would have been my first venture.
CA You develop property in the region of the Moreton Bay (Regional) Council; correct?
W That's correct.
CA How many have you done within the Moreton Bay area?
W I'm not entirely sure of the number –
CA A lot?
W – of developments. Yes, it is quite a lot. Two years ago we celebrated a 20th anniversary and it was in excess of 5500 lots in Moreton Bay in my twenty years.
CA Is it fair to say that you develop, in the main, in the Moreton Bay area?
W Currently, yes.
CA Is there some reason you choose to develop in that area?
W It's my home patch of where I've grown up.
CA What area did you grow up in, Mr Trask?
W Started in Redcliffe, then Kallangur, and then back to Redcliffe.
CA Do you develop there because it's somewhere you're familiar with, is that the way it works?
W I obviously have a familiarity with the area, but I also like to be able to drive to all my projects in one day.

CA What kinds of developments have you done? Can you give us an idea of the nature and scale of what you do?

W Oh, typically anything residential. Typically I'll buy, you know, a paddock off a farmer or a mum and dad that are, you know, ready to down-size, and run the approval processes, run the operational works processes, build the roads and all the infrastructure that is associated with a land development. I've done townhouses which were for personal investment where I bought a piece of land, ran an approval process, and then employed a builder for the task of undertaking construction.

CA You mentioned you might typically commence with a paddock and develop infrastructure on it.

W Mmm-hmm.

CA How frequently do you proceed to the next stage of developing dwellings and so forth on land that you have put infrastructure on?

W Generally speaking – I'm not a builder so I don't undertake the actual house-building activity as such.

CA Does that style of development bring you into contact with the Moreton Regional Council to get approvals and so forth?

W Yes.

CA With what regularity?

W Weekly.

CA Do you have any political affiliation? Are you a member of any party?

W No.

CA You know the Mayor of Moreton (Bay) Regional Council, Mr Allan Sutherland; correct?
W Yes.
CA For how long have you known him?
W I knew of him as a person right back to my early days when I was a mechanic, when I worked at Sundown Marine, that was a local marine dealer, and then more recently in – it was either 2001 or 2002, something like that, when we took Redcliffe Council to court for a subdivision approval that wasn't satisfactory.
CA Did you become friendly with him?
W I like to think I'm friendly with most of the people that I deal with.
CA Is he a friend of yours?
W I class him as a friend now, yes.
CA You socialise?
W Yes.
CA In what way?
W We go fishing. We'll catch up for a drink.
CA Do you visit each other's houses?
W Yes.
CA Would you see him with some frequency, some regularity?
W I wouldn't say that there's any regularity to it, it's sporadic. We do try to go away on fishing trips at least once a year.
CA You have given some assistance to at least a couple of his election campaigns?
W Yes.

CA Was 2012 the first of those that you helped him with?

W I'm not 100 per cent on the dates. The first election campaign that I helped him financially was the original amalgamation campaign.

CA I think that would be 2008, does that sound right?

W Possibly, mate.

CA You don't know?

W It's stretching too far back. I don't remember that detail.

   (A $100,000 donation was a detail, a memorable one, you would have thought.)

CA But you recall an amalgamation.

W I know that I supported him for the amalgamation.

CA What was the nature of the assistance you gave him for the amalgamation election?

W A donation.

CA Just a donation?

W Mmm-hmm.

CA Did you do any soliciting of donations of anyone else?

W I don't recall.

CA You do recall a donation?

W Yes.

CA Is that the only thing that you recall by way of assistance to him?

W I remember meeting with him and discussing what he saw as a way forward in terms of the amalgamation of the council.

CA Was your support based on friendship or based on what he told you about what he intended to do, or both?

W I met with other candidates that were running for that election and, out of all of the candidates that I met with, he was the only person who had a plan for how to amalgamate three councils together and continue a business as usual position for the council.

(Mayor Sutherland delivered his first post-amalgamation Budget a few months after the election. Cr Sutherland said any council staff who did not share his vision should get out straight away.

Cr Sutherland's Mayoral salary roughly tripled on amalgamation. Other councillors had their salaries rise by between 50 and 100 per cent.

One of the promises of amalgamation was cost saving. One council worker I spoke to did not receive a promotion during 12 years of service, pre and post-amalgamation. Her efficiency was rewarded with more responsibilities for the same pay. 'We decided this council did not give a shit about staff,' she told me. 'I decided, for my sanity, I could afford to get out. Others decided they couldn't.' During her 12th year, she got out.

Unsuccessful 2016 Division 3 candidate Kimberly James received $30,000 in donations from the union, the CMFEU, when she promised to investigate treatment of council staff if she was elected.)

CA And in addition to that, he was a friend of yours?

W He was an associate at that point in time. I'd say that I've, you know, developed more of a friendship with him since that time.
CA The support that you gave him, was that a reflection of the style of vision that he had for the amalgamated council?
W He was the only person that had a plan on how to bring three councils together.
CA Moving forward to the (2012) election after that, which is the one before the one last year –
W Yes.
CA – do you recall whether you made a donation for his campaign expenses on that occasion?
W I did, yes.
CA Was there any other assistance that you can recall –
W Not that I recall.
CA - To his campaign?
W Not that I recall.
CA Did you, like, network on his behalf, approach other potential donors; that kind of thing?
W Sorry, I was involved with a function at Lakeside Raceway.
CA What was that?
W That was a fundraiser.
CA Were you there as an attendee or some more proactive capacity?
W A more proactive capacity.
CA To be specific, trying to secure donations, was that part of it or not?

W Not necessarily to try and secure donations but I was instrumental in the setting up of the day and, you know, organising the basics of a fundraising event. You know, it's not something that I've done before so I wouldn't say that it's something, you know, I'm familiar with.
CA That was your first one?
W Yes. And the last.
CA Okay. How did you come to get that job?
W I'm a member of the UDIA which is a peak industry body. And it was something that as a committee at that particular time was discussed at a committee meeting and –

(UDIA stands for Urban Development Institute Australia. CCC hearing witnesses Mr Trask and Tim Connolly are on the Moreton Bay Management Committee.)
CA To conduct this fundraiser?
W To conduct a fundraiser, yes.
CA Right.
W And I'm not entirely sure how it spawned into a day at Lakeside but I thought it was a good idea because I am a car enthusiast.
CA Was Councillor Sutherland involved in the decision to conduct that fundraising day?
W I couldn't tell you.

(There appears to have been two fundraising days at Lakeside, one in 2011 and another in 2012.)
CA You don't recall having any discussion with him about it?
W No.

CA Did he attend?
W Yes.
CA Going forward to the 2016 election or the campaign, at least, did you offer some assistance to Mayor Sutherland for that campaign?
W Yes.
CA He was by then, would you say, friendly with you?
W Yes.
CA Had been for really a number of years?
W Yes.
CA Did you make a donation towards his campaign in 2016?
W Yes.
CA Would you take on some role of approaching others for donations?
W Yes.
CA Can you tell us what you did?
W Rang up some people that I do business with and asked them to kick the can for money.

(Rattle the can, kick the can; this can is getting thoroughly battered and it has to hold $100,000.)

CA People you do business with, in the same kind of business as you?
W Yes.
CA Developers?
W Not necessarily developers, but marketers and builders more so.
CA Were you successful?
W Yes.
CA Got some donations for the Mayor?

W Yes.
CA Do you know of Moreton Futures Trust?
W Yes, I do.
CA When did you first hear about its existence, do you remember? Just in terms of the election campaigns, was it the latest one or the one before?
W No, the one prior.
CA What did you learn about it?
W Not a great deal.
CA Tell us what you learned about it, even if it's not a great deal?
W I understood it was, you know, a third party vessel. I don't know how you'd describe it adequately, but a third party vessel that was there for the purpose of collecting funds for, you know, political candidates for the purpose of paying their expenditure and so forth on campaigning costs.
CA Did that have anything to do with Mayor Sutherland as far as you knew?
W It was an option for donors to send money to the Moreton Futures for the purpose of his campaign, yes.
CA Do you know who administered the trust?
W At that particular time, no.
CA Did you later learn?
W Only as a result of reading the transcripts of this hearing.
CA Having done so, perhaps you now know the name Kirby Leeke?
W Yes, correct.
CA Have you ever spoken to him?

W Yes, I have.
CA For what purpose?
W For the purpose of arranging donations to be deposited to the trust account.
CA For the 2016 campaign?
W That's correct.
CA How did you come to be in contact with him?
W I was given his name as the –
CA Do you recall who gave it to you?
W No, I don't recall.
CA You were given his name?
W Given his name.
CA In what connection?
W As the contact with regard to Moreton Futures Trust.
CA That led to some contact between you and him?
W Yes.
CA And what was the content of that?
W Just a telephone call to ask his address to drop cheques off.
CA Just one phone call?
W Yes.
CA To find out where to take cheques to?
W There may have been others but I don't recall.
CA Did you talk with him at all about the way the trust operated, whether the Mayor might benefit, any of that kind of thing?
W In one of the conversations he told me it was preferable if money was being deposited to the account, that there were wishes as to who the funds were to benefit.

CA   Conversation with whom are you speaking about?
W Myself.
CA Yes, and who?
W Kirby Leeke.
CA And tell me again what did he tell you?
W Just when there were funds to be deposited to the Moreton Futures Trust, who those funds were preferred to benefit.
CA Well, did you give any funds to Mr Leeke to be applied to the Moreton Futures Trust?
W Myself personally?
CA Yes.
W I believe I did, yes.
CA Your own donation, was that made to the trust or to the Mayor himself?
W There were donations that I sent directly to the Mayor and I think that there was a donation to the Moreton Futures Trust as well.
CA Did you convey anything to Kirby Leeke about who you would prefer would benefit from Moreton Futures Trust money?
W Yes.
CA What did you say?
W Well, for Allan Sutherland.

   (That rather defeats the purpose of a trust when Mr Trask could have given more money to Cr Sutherland directly.)
CA Do you recall having any discussion with the Mayor in the course of the 2016 campaign about the operation of this Moreton Futures Trust?

W Wouldn't have.

CA No?

W Wouldn't have. Wouldn't have a reason to.

CA Did you have any reason to suggest to donors that they might make a donation via this trust as opposed to just giving the money to the Mayor?

W We told them they had a choice between Moreton Futures Trust or directly to Allan. Moreton Futures Trust, in my mind, as I suggested to them, was a better vessel because it was a third party. It was a trust. I was aware that Kirby Leeke was an accountant and that provided an accountancy function for Allan with respect to him not having to deal with the money directly.

CA There was the accountancy function. There was also some attraction in Moreton Futures Trust being a third party as you have described?

W Yes.

CA What was the attraction of that so far as you were concerned?

W Oh, some people are touchy about, you know, politicians receiving donations. I've already been hung out to dry in the press enough, so it didn't worry me anymore.

(People in the development industry avoiding public disclosure of donations is definitely an inappropriate use of a trust. As for Mr Trask being hung out to dry, unless he can show evidence, I suggest he exaggerates his suffering of the slings and arrows of outrageous media.)

CA The options that you gave to donors, did they come from your own thought processes or were they suggested to you by someone, either by the Mayor or someone on behalf of the Mayor?
W No, it's mine – my thought process.
CA I'll just show you a list. It will come up on the screen. Do you see that list, Mr Trask?
W Yes.
CA There is a list of names in the first column. Do you recognise any of those organisations?
W Yes.
CA As being organisations that you approached for the purpose of making donations?
W Yes.
CA On behalf of the Mayor's campaign?
W Yes.
CA Tell us which ones you had some interaction with to try to get some donations?
W Phillip Usher, Sunvista, Impact and Open Corp Project Management.
CA You knew representatives of each of those companies?
W Correct.
CA And had some discussion with such representatives?
W Yes.
CA To try to get donations?
W Yep.
CA And apparently did so, according to this list?
W Yep.

19

PAUL PISASALE (pronounced Pis-ar-lee) resigned as Ipswich Mayor on June 6, 2017, in a hospital gown and in hospital after he said his chronic condition of multiple sclerosis had worsened. It was a day after Queensland CCC officers and police raided his home and council offices.

Mr Pisasale was later charged with extortion and assault, though in an unusual action, authorities sealed the details of the charges from public view. Some might have thought it funny that, soon after that, the details of historical child-sex charges against Catholic Cardinal George Pell were sealed in Melbourne.

Continuing media reports on Paul Pisasale have a fondness for reproducing a photo of the former Mayor in his hospital gown.

After hearing of the charges, Council CEO Jim Lindsay said it was business as normal for Ipswich council.

Mr Pisasale received more votes than any other Queensland mayor at the 2016 election where he polled more than 80 per cent of the vote.

Councillor Pisasale was first elected Mayor in 2004, four years after I finished working for the *Queensland Times* newspaper group. He and his brother Charlie were both on Ipswich City Council when I was writing for the heavy transport newspaper *Big Rigs*. Paul Pisasale was first elected to Council in 1991. The oldest of three Pisasale brothers, Charlie, was elected to Ipswich Council in 1995. From 1995 to 2004, John Nugent was Mayor of Ipswich.

In 2010 Mayor Pisasale was a national finalist as Australia's Local Hero, part of the Australian of the Year Awards.

His nomination read in part:

'As Mayor of Ipswich and President of the Urban Local Government Association, Paul Pisasale has a deep loyalty for his city and Queensland. . . . He has always served his community in one way or another and was the driving force behind the formation of the Young Unemployed People of Ipswich, assisting unemployed people to gain work skills and employment.

Paul also established the Ipswich and Moreton Regional Development Corporation which helped businesses develop and reshape the city. Paul has worked to protect existing parklands and create a new nature centre where visitors can see rare and protected species. Under Paul's leadership, Ipswich can boast an award for the world's most liveable mid-sized city and a World Environment Day Award for excellence in environmental management.

Cr Pisasale won a place in the Guinness Book of World Records in 2008, for the world's biggest collection of short-black coffee cups in what are known as demitasse sets. He took the world record with 650 sets but the number more than doubled as people learned about it and donated towards it. The donations include coffee mugs, some quite large. To my untrained eye, these are decidedly dodgy if they are being passed off as traditional vessels for short blacks.

The collection is on public display and Ipswich Council has housed it in many glass and timber display cabinets.

Mr Pisasale owns it and has declared it in his interests register as being valued at more than $5000. In 2013, Mr Pisasale said it was worth more than $100,000, a nice drop of short black indeed.

Transcript #11
Abridged by Bernie Dowling

Witness Paul Pisasale, April 19, 2017
PO, Presiding Officer Alan MacSporran QC
CA, Counsel Assisting, Glen Rice QC
W, Paul Pisasale

PO Mr Rice.
CA Mr Chairman, the first witness to be called is Mr Paul Pisasale, the Mayor of the Ipswich City Council. I call Paul John Pisasale.
PO Thank you. Good morning, Mr Pisasale. How are you?
W Good morning.

CA Sir, is your name Paul John Pisasale?
W Correct.
CA You're the Mayor of Ipswich City Council?
W Yes.
CA Mr Pisasale, in the 2016 elections, you were returned, I think, for your fourth term as Mayor?
W That's correct.
CA Having been first elected as Mayor in 2004?
W Yes.
CA I think in the last election you had a very high percentage of votes in your favour; is that right?
W That's correct.
CA What's the figure?
W In the whole four elections.
CA What are the figures?
W Oh, about 85 per cent.
CA In each one?
W Yes. The average over the four years was about 85.
CA You are a member of the Labor Party, are you not?
W Correct.
CA For how long have you been a member?
W Oh, 25 years or more.
CA For the purpose of election campaigning, do you run as an independent candidate?
W Yes, I do.
CA Is that how you describe yourself for campaign purposes?
W Not for campaign purposes. For the way I run my existence as Mayor.
CA For all purposes?

W For all purposes.

CA Can you give us your view on what that notion of independence means, when everyone knows, really, that you're a long-term member of the Labor Party?

W Yes, I'm a long-term member of the Labor Party, but it has no influence and has not had any influence in regards how I run my job, because as people know that I work and my role as the Mayor of Ipswich is to represent the city, and to represent the city I need to work at all levels of government, and I need to work with people who are of all political parties, and I do that.

CA As a very senior participant in the process, can I just ask you your view on whether you think party membership, or other forms of obvious alignment to a party, should be known to electors in the course of an election campaign?

W Yes, correct, but mine has been in my register of interests since the day I was elected.

CA Likewise, what would your view be on whether funding from a party or sources close to a party should be made known by a candidate in the course of a campaign?

W Not only just political donations, but all donations should be known.

CA In the course of a campaign, though?

W Yes, correct.

CA In the way the system has operated, the disclosure return is lodged perhaps some months after the election is held?

W Not necessarily. I have a register of interests, and I also include all my gifts or any donations in that register of interests as well, before the election.

CA Just perhaps if you wouldn't mind explaining, then, what this register of interests is and how you contribute information to it in the course of a campaign?

W Well, not only in the course of a campaign. In your role as Mayor, if you do receive any gifts or donations or lunches or hospitality, we have a register of interests that gets checked on a regular basis, that you have to upgrade within six weeks of receiving that gift.

(The register must be updated within 30 days not six weeks. 'Should a councillor become aware that their register of interests, or the register of interests of a related person, no longer contains the correct particulars, they need to ensure that the register is updated within 30 days after they become aware of the correct particulars.')

CA Is that maintained by the Electoral Commission?

W No, it's a council document. I think it's maintained by the – it's just been audited by the Queensland Government. It's a Queensland Government document.

CA And is it available for public inspection?

W It's online.

CA On, what, the Ipswich City Council website?

W Correct.

CA And do you, as and when you receive gifts, as you do, have a practice concerning the updating of that register?

W Yes. I have a regular monthly procedure where I upgrade it all the time.

CA Is that register applicable also to other councillors?

W Yes.

CA And do other councillors follow the same process as you by way of updating it, do you know?

W Well, I wouldn't know what other councillors do.

CA You don't know. But do you know whether there is a register maintained by other councillors?

W Oh, they have to be. It's part of the process.

CA And you don't make it your business to check on whether they're updating it –

W No, I don't. I've got enough to do.

CA Okay. And is that register to be completed by councillors?

W Correct.

CA What about candidates to be councillors in the course of an election campaign – does that have any relevance to them?

W No.

CA Do you know what a group of candidates constitutes under the Local Government Electoral Act?

W Yes, I think so.

CA Can you give us your understanding of it?

W Well, a group of candidates that form together to form a team. They have common values and common policies and run as a team.
CA Have you ever done so?
W No.
CA What about voting on council, is there any bloc voting on council that you've observed?
W No.
CA Even though, for example, you and Mr Tully are both long-term members of the Labor Party and have that obvious philosophical alignment?
W Not if you see us in council.
CA I beg your pardon?
W Not if you see us in council. We've had a number of debates.
CA We've made mention so far of disclosure returns. I'd just like to ask you a little bit about those and show you yours, to begin with. Just have a look at this. Just confirm that that's a copy of your disclosure return for the 2016 election?
W Yes.
CA As a general matter, is it important to you to know who your donors are so that perceptions of electors can be managed about who is giving you money?
W Yes.
CA And given that you update this register of interests or register of gifts from time to time, does that keep you up to date on who's giving you money?
W Correct.

CA So far as these returns are concerned, can I ask you your view about whether the disclosure returns serve the purpose of informing electors, given that they're completed and furnished to the Electoral Commission some months after the election?
W Yes, I don't make the rules, but it would be a lot better to have them all, you know, put in before the election.
CA Yes. Well, you received quite a large sum in donations over the disclosure period for this return; correct?
W Yes, just enough to run the election.
CA Well, it was about $220,000?
W Correct.
CA So is that what you spent?
W Yes.
CA And the make-up of that amount involved contributions from quite a large number of donors, in fact 76 in total; correct?
W Correct.
CA Given that there's such a large number of donors to you, how do you identify and manage conflicts of interest with respect to the interests of the donors as compared with your function as Mayor?
W I don't understand the question. You're saying that in council – if a matter comes up with council, where someone has made a donation, I declare an interest in that particular item.
CA Having done so, do you continue to deliberate or vote on the matter under consideration?
W In what respect?

CA Well –
W A planning matter?
CA Well, for example.
W Well, there's been about – if you look at the planning documents, there would have been about, say – I looked at the records - about 800 planning matters and this has been investigated by the CCC before, and only two of those went to council.

(Some might suggest that delegating 798 out of 800 planning decisions to unelected officers might not be democratic best practice. In Moreton Bay Regional Council, decisions are declared code assessable – more straight-forward – or impact – on the community – assessable. Almost all code assessable developments are approved by council public servants. Divisional councillors can also request code assessable applications to be approved by full council. Impact assessable developments are almost always approved by full council.

As I said before, it is my understanding Councillors have had a lot more input into Ipswich development decisions than indicated by Cr Pisasale or Cr Tully.)

CA Are you saying that so far as Ipswich City Council is concerned, a conflict of interest with developers is not a big issue?

W - No, we make sure that any conflict of interest is reported, and we make sure that the officers have the right to do their job without any interference from a political –

CA How do you make sure that any conflict of interest is reported?

W Well, you report in council. If the matter comes up, it's recorded in due course of the council process or committee system.

CA Well, the onus is on whom to raise it?

W The onus is on yourself.

(It will interesting to see if the State Government enacts the CCC suggestions of changes to resolution of conflicts of interest.

'After a councillor declares a conflict of interest, or where another councillor has reported the councillor's conflict of interest, other persons entitled to vote at the meeting are required to decide: (a) whether the councillor has a real or perceived conflict of interest in the matter (b) whether the councillor should leave the meeting room and stay out of the meeting room while the matter is being discussed and voted on, or whether the councillor should remain in the meeting room to discuss and vote on the matter.

'The views put forward by each other person and the final decision of the group should be recorded in the minutes of the meeting.'

Another recommendation would require any councillor who knows or reasonably suspects that another councillor has a conflict of interest or material personal interest to report this to the person presiding over the meeting or the Chief Executive Officer of the council.

Penalties for councillors who fail to comply with their obligations regarding conflicts of interest could include removal from office.

Moreton Bay Regional Council meeting minutes are scant at the best of times so it would be quite a departure to have councillors record their reasons for a decision regarding conflicts of interest.)

CA So there's an element of trust so far as you and any other councillor who may have received a donation to make the declaration of that conflict of interest?

W That's correct. The issue is that councillors and Mayors have to run a campaign and they don't receive funding like other levels of government, and somehow you have to raise the money to run a proper campaign to keep your community informed. It would be better to have it as the same level – same rules for all levels of government.

CA Well, that raises another question, of how funding ought best be done for local government, such as Ipswich City Council?

W I'd say we'd just use the same process as they do in state and federal, so the onus is not on councillors and Mayor to find the money to run a proper campaign. The most important thing in any campaign is that the people know what you stand for for the next four years.

CA Funding of that kind, though, would really be contingent on party-political endorsements, wouldn't it, and running of tickets, and so forth?

W I don't think so.

CA No. How would you see it working?

W Well, if you want to be a true independent, you've got to raise your own money. There was no political donations to my campaign at all.

CA But if the same rules applied to state and federal campaigns, they are substantially funded by the parties that run them?

W No, not necessarily. There's a lot of good independents that run at state and federal level.

CA What would be your preferred, if you could explain, funding model for local government in Ipswich?

W I'd say my preferred funding model is to have the same, where people got a payment on the amount of votes they got, similar to state and federal. That way, people can then run their own campaigns without having to put pressure on the poor old developer, who gives because they want good leadership in the city and then gets sort of accused of trying to buy a vote. You know, I always have a simple statement I make: people give to churches, but they don't expect divine intervention.

(Actually people do expect divine intervention when they donate to churches, and here on earth, too. It is a favourite Pisasale analogy but not particularly apposite.)

CA You mentioned developers. Is that your view of why developers make donations to councillors – looking for good government, or is there –

W Well, I'd say so. Out of all that money, only about 15 per cent was from the development industry. The other was from hardworking people and the people of Ipswich who appreciate what I do.

CA Would you perceive, so far as developers again, to use them as an example, there's any perception that giving a donation might benefit them in some way?

W It just - no, it won't, because we've got great planners in the City of Ipswich, and I can tell you that the planning people are not going to be bought off by a developer. They are professional people and they'll be making the decisions that are in the best interests of that planning document and the city.

CA Does the fact that a business or individual has made a contribution, as set out in your disclosure return, give such a person any preferential access to you?

W No, not really. I'm available 24/7 on the phone and many people ring me, whether they've given me money or not.

CA So from your perspective, it's not a case of their getting any benefit from you?

W No, not really. To be honest with you, I couldn't even list who gave to me because there were so many of them, and I had a team of people that were there to support me, and they ran all that.

CA It rather gets back to what I asked you before. There are so many donors, and I think you've just acknowledged, that you lose track of who they are?

W Yes.

CA It raises the question, I suggest to you, of how you identify any conflicts of interest when you even forget who your donors are?

W No, because at the end of the day if it's something coming up from council, I always check my register. I always do that. I have staff checking that because we're very meticulous on that, because it's one of those issues that are important to me because I don't want to cause any problem to them as well. But, at the end of the day, I treat everybody equal, whether they've given or not. I treat all political parties exactly the same, and that's why our city is going well.

CA Mr Chairman, I was going to ask for a short break for the time being. There's some information that has been received that may or may not lead to some more questions for Mr Pisasale and we just need a little time to sort that out.

PO Yes. Mr Pisasale, you would be aware that there was some material that we had requested from you, which we only received reasonably late in the piece. I am not being critical, but it is the fact that we have only just received that, so we need a little bit of time to look at that, and it seems desirable we do that now while you're here –

W Yes.

PO – rather than stand you down and bring you back on another occasion.

W That's okay.

PO I understand you have, as is obvious, many commitments outside this hearing. With your indulgence, we will adjourn briefly to let my Counsel

Assisting and legal staff look at some of these documents, in an endeavour to try and finish you this morning, to let you get on your way.

W I'd appreciate that.

(Mr Pisasale's Sicilian ancestors might not have appreciated being told that someone was going to finish them this morning. Please pardon the ethnic stereotyping in my pursuit of levity.)

PO All right. We will just adjourn for a period, and, Mr Rice, you can let me know when you're ready to resume, if you would.

SHORT ADJOURNMENT

PO Mr Rice, are you ready to proceed?
CA Yes, thank you. Thanks for waiting, Mr Pisasale.
W That's okay.
CA There is a feature of the processing of payments for your campaign expenses that the Commission would like you to shed such light on as you can.
W Yes.
CA You know of a company called Zimmi Group?
W Correct.
CA It's your daughter's company, correct?
W Correct.
CA Her name is Lisa?
W Yes.
CA Did you know that it was incorporated in September of 2015?
W Yes.

CA She is the only director and the only shareholder; correct?
W I'm – I think so.
CA At any rate, without that kind of detail, you know that that's effectively her company?
W Yes, yes. Yes, of course.
CA She had a significant role by way of assistance in your campaign; would that be right?
W Yes.
CA Could you explain what her role was?
W Look, I went and saw Lisa because I – my role as Mayor entitled me to do my job as Mayor right up till the election, which I had a lot of work to do, so I asked her if she would take over and run my campaign on a professional basis.

(It is not correct that Mr Pisasale was entitled to act as Mayor until election day. Council is prorogued before an election and Council and mayoral positions are suspended. After the prorogue it is an offence for the Mayor or councillors to use the services available to their offices for campaign purposes. The administration of council is placed in the hands of the CEO and their delegates.)

W After a bit of deliberation, she said she'd only do it on one condition, and that was that if I kept out of it. I agreed to that and I said to her that I want to employ her company to run a professional campaign, and she said she would do that because – I employed her because I believe she is one of the best in the industry. And so she ran the campaign, and ran it well and made it very, very professional, and, at the same time, I was able to continue to do my job as Mayor right up to the election.

CA Could you tell us, then – you mentioned she is the best in the business, in your view.

W Yes.

CA What was her skill-set that she could bring to the task?

W Well, she's marketing, design, you know, digital media space. She was able to bring fresh young eyes to, you know, usually a boring campaign. And the colours she used – not necessarily what I would have chosen, and I was really pleased at the type of design. She brought – her experience in New York and where she's been had really brought new eyes to our campaign.

CA She purchased a lot of campaign material for the campaign; correct?

W Correct, yes.

CA And in the first instance, tell me if this is correct, she arranged for suppliers to invoice her company, Zimmi Group, for such materials and other products –

W That's right. Her company –

CA – for your campaign purposes?

W It was her company running the campaign and she would then supply the invoices to the campaign office, and I had two people that separately had to verify the payments and the cheques.

CA She would engage suppliers, who would invoice her company?

W Correct.

CA And then she, or at least her company, would prepare an invoice from Zimmi Group to your mayoral campaign fund?
W Correct.
CA That's how it worked?
W Yes.
CA Could I show you three invoices from Zimmi Group, which have some supplier invoices stapled to them? Just take a moment, Mr Pisasale, to have a look.
W I just haven't got my glasses. It's not huge print.
CA I see, all right. Could you tell me this: in your capacity, at the level you operate at, being the mayoral candidate, is it likely that you would see invoices of this kind?
W Me?
CA You, yes.
W No, this is the first I've seen these.
CA Okay, you probably don't need your glasses to tell us that much, that you haven't seen any of that material –
W No.
CA – before today?
W No.
CA In the first instance, you rely on your daughter to engage the suppliers for the product or service that's needed?
W I had a good team organising all this and they knew what the rules were –
CA Yes.
W – and they made sure they abided by all the rules.

CA Well, were you aware that these instances that I have shown you of invoices from Zimmi Group to your mayoral campaign show a significant mark-up in the cost of the service as invoiced to Zimmi Group –

W Yes.

CA -- and then passed on to your mayoral campaign?

W That mark-up is her wages and her costs in delivering it. She stopped her company work and I employed her as full time to do this. So she was operating under the same rules as she runs her company.

CA Did she not also bill the mayoral campaign for hours of work?

W Yes, but they weren't the significant hours that she put in. There was a lot of times that she didn't bill, so she did bill some hours, yes, that's correct.

CA Well, as a general proposition, then, were you aware that there was a mark-up –

W Yes. It's like normal company practice, correct.

CA I see.

W Because the mark-up – you got the goods. The design, and all the work that goes in to getting those goods which I couldn't do it and other people couldn't do it, so that's the cost in regards to the mark-up, it's her time and her effort, or the company's time, to deliver that.

CA Did you have any agreement with her as to any formula that might be applied –

W No.

CA – or was it up to her to apply just commercial principles?

W I told her to use full commercial principles because I didn't want any favours and I didn't want her company or herself to miss out. But I know that she put many hours and weekends and nights into it that she didn't bill.

CA Was there anyone scrutinising the level of mark-up from her company to the mayoral campaign?

W I'd say so.

CA Who?

W Well, the people that would get the invoices would have asked.

CA Do you know – well –

W I don't know what you're suggesting in regards to mark-up. That's just normal commercial practices. Are you saying they're unfair?

CA I'm just asking you about it, Mr Pisasale.

W Well, I wouldn't even know what the mark-ups are, but I did give her riding instructions to run it as a proper business in a proper professional manner.

CA Can I suggest this to you, that a preliminary analysis of $108,000 worth of campaign expenses shows a mark-up by Zimmi Group to your mayoral campaign of about $32,000?

20

QUEENSLAND MAYORS have too much power and not enough accountability. They can appoint CEOs (within a process they can dominate) and annually review the performance of CEOs. Mayors can intimidate, punish and reward councillors, and hire and fire public servants. Not only can mayors do these things, they do. Who's to stop them? Not a compliant media whose journalists they reward with regular meetings, off-the-record gossip, and pretence of friendship. Not the public servants, frightened of the consequences of whistleblowing and who, if it all becomes too much, can walk away, and perhaps seek work in another council. That's if they are not blackballed when one CEO talks to another to warn of a trouble maker. Not the ratepayer who only gets the chance once every four years to remove a mayor, and then has to hope a better choice bobs up.

It's not co-incidental that the candidate who spends the most money campaigning ends up as mayor. Unfortunately, who pays the piper calls the tune and the band beating time in local government is marching from the big end of town down Development Road.

I would like to see changes to how we elect mayors and how they function. I am realist enough to know good ideas always struggle against the inertia of the political process but it is a start to have people discussing change which is a long and winding road.

Prime Minister Malcolm Turnbull and Opposition Leader Bill Shorten recently appeared to have a meeting of the minds on the virtues of four-year fixed parliamentary terms. I first raised this idea from a Bribie Island resident in my weekly humour column in 2004.

Daniel Williams wanted a regular electoral cycle. I quote from my column which you can find in my collection of seven years of columns, *7 Shouts*.

'Daniel says one election should be held each year on the following basis:
* Year 1 local government (council);
* Year 2 state;
* Year 3 Federal House of Representatives; and
* Year 4 Federal half-Senate
– My Shout, February 27, 2004'

Over the years, I promoted what I called the dannymander in a number of columns and Mr Williams reached out to Federal parliamentarians. Maybe our humble efforts were tiny signposts on the road to change.

The reforms to local government I am proposing are in the context of councils for which political parties do not run. Contrary to general opinion I believe ratepayers are better served by councils where parties do hold sway as it dilutes power. In 'independent' councils, much power falls to the mayor and the CEO.

If a council is independent, why does a mayor need to have considerable say on hiring and firing CEOs and other public servants? At a state and federal level, you expect slaughter of politically aligned department heads after a change of government. At a practical level, what skills does a mayor bring to the table where the discussion is about the high-end administrative skills of CEOs and department heads? What price fearless and independent advice being given by a public servant to a mayor who has the staffer's destiny in their hands? That price could be and has been your job.

While the mayor is usually only one person in the selection process for CEO, from my limited experience, they usually get the one they want. I cannot see any downside to removing a mayor from the selection process. The mayor's role would be to offer general advice and opinion on expected community outcomes from the offices of CEO and department heads. Similarly, a mayor should not be able to fire a public servant.

I believe a mayor should be elected by their fellow councillors. This is a sensible reform which would be rejected by most as an affront to democracy. But the Prime Minister and Premiers are elected by a section of their party membership. A mayor being elected from councillors would then serve a designated geographical area, called by such names as divisions or wards. The Prime Minister of Australia is representing the residents of Wentworth so it seems an anomaly a mayor is exempt from similar duties. A mayor could be allowed extra administrative assistance to assist the ratepayers of their division. The ceremonial responsibilities now undertaken by a mayor could be delegated more to other councillors. A mayor should not be allowed to serve more than two terms. Mayors and deputy mayors would receive higher salaries than other councillors but the disparity would not be as much as it is now.

21

IN AUSTRALIA, we make excuses for politicians caught breaking the law. 'They all do it,' is a common one. When you think about it, that's a frightening excuse which suggests corruption is endemic and it is not such a big deal anyway. When a federal politician is caught out rorting their expense account, the immediate reaction is to call for another inquiry. The fault lies in our systems, it can't be in our political stars.

I have zero sympathy for public officials who are on a good wicket financially yet feel the need to thrust their fingers into the cookie jar. I am all for reviewing public policy and definitely in favour of public CCC hearings and a federal Independent Commissioner Against Corruption (ICAC) but I would also like to see a few politicians put in jail to concentrate the minds of those free on doing the right thing.

As LGAQ CEO Greg Hallam told the Operation Belcarra hearings, good public policy is one that you can enforce and one that improves the system. He might have added the Benthamite rider that it creates the greatest good for the public as a whole. It is for the general good not for that of the favoured group of developers, business people, consultants, and lobbyists.

Here are what I believe are worthwhile reforms of council elections and governance of councils and governments in general.

Most are self-explanatory for readers who have progressed this far into my book.

- Tighten up third-party political donations so the receiver must know who donated to the third party.
- Ban donations of one candidate to another candidate's campaign.
- Have real-time declaration of political donations. Real time could mean as little as within a day of receipt. Donors could declare within a day of delivering a gift. If you must have a longer period such as seven business days, donors and candidates must not give or receive donations within eight business days of an election.
- Introduce fines for violations of the Electoral Act and undergo prosecutions in cases of suspected serious infringements.
- Have compulsory meetings where candidates learn of their obligations under the Electoral Act. These are explained comprehensively in plain English before an informational USB stick is provided to take away.
- Councils must create an election website in which candidates can provide a profile and policy statements. The administration of the website should be outsourced.

- Investigate fair but frugal public funding of council candidates.
- Investigate mechanisms for more women and ethnic diversity on council.
- Ban councillors from developing or conducting a business which interfaces with their Council.
- Introduce mechanisms to decrease the instances of closed sessions of council. Define more clearly why a meeting should be closed.
- Minute all council workshops and other private meetings which derive recommendations for co-oordination committee meetings. These minutes should be made public.
- Make all meetings of councillors, other than workshops, public. Video all council meetings for transmission on the internet.
- Disallow councils from setting up private companies with less onerous disclosure provisions than other council bodies.
- Hold an investigation into council rates and alternative forms of council income. Council rates are increasing significantly above the rate of inflation. If this continues, it will impose heavy financial burdens on some home owners and businesses.
- Consider adopting a system advocated by Dr Cameron Murray where development land is taxed on a successful material change of use (MCU) which increases the value of the land.

- Make councillors part-time and eligible for only two terms. From the savings, more councillors can be hired.
- Councillors elect mayors from within their ranks.
- Enhance the protection of whistle-blowers. This is a real challenge, not being addressed in Australia. If a whistle-blower's identity is uncovered, their employment and health prospects are in jeopardy.
- Introduce a federal Independent Commissioner Against Corruption (ICAC.)

Good people elected to public office can turn bad without their realising it. It usually happens over time when hubris sets in. Supporters pat them on the back. They isolate themselves by screening complaints. They declare critics to be trouble makers.

After a few years, they convince themselves they are doing such a sterling job they deserve a few more perks than the terms of their remuneration provide. And, of course, they know it is only justice they are returned to office at election times. They must do everything in their power to ensure the voter makes the right decision and ticks their box.

As the Federal Parliament is the most sophisticated in the land, a Federal ICAC would set the example for other legislatures that corruption will be exposed and dealt with.

22

A FEW EXPERTS were called before the CCC hearing to clarify issues and suggest remedies for problems in electoral and donation laws and procedures.

One of these was Professor Graeme Orr who had patiently explained the relevant laws to us when my colleague, Walter Burns, and I were investigating Moreton Futures Trust in 2015. We found him a most practical person as well as an intellectual.

Graeme Orr is Professor at the University of Queensland TC Beirne School of Law.

The law school website explains his considerable credits.

'The law of politics, in particular electoral law, is Professor Graeme Orr's primary research expertise. He has authored *The Law of Politics* (2010) and *Ritual and Rhythm in Electoral Systems* (2015), co-authored *The Law of Deliberative Democracy* (2016), co-edited *Realising Democracy* (2003) and *Electoral Democracy: Australian Prospects* (2011) and three symposia on the law of politics (in the *Griffith Law Review* (1998), the *Federal Law Review* (2004) and the *Election Law Journal* 2013)). His doctoral thesis explored the nature and regulation of electoral bribery.

Graeme's current projects include work with Ron Levy on deliberative approaches to the law of democracy. He is also beginning a new project on 'horizontal censorship' – the ability of employers, social media and others to restrain 'free speech' by using their contractual and property law power, to defend their own 'brand' or right to dissociate themselves from a speaker.'

ONE of the things Professor Orr advised us of in 2015 was the obligation of beneficiaries of an unincorporated trust such as Moreton Futures to know who the trustees were.

Transcript #12
Abridged by Bernie Dowling

Witness Professor Graeme Orr, April 19, 2017
PO, Presiding Officer Alan MacSporran QC
CA, Counsel Assisting, Glen Rice QC
W, Graeme Orr

CA Is your name Graeme Orr?
W That's me, yes.
CA You're a professor of law and you occupy that position at the University of Queensland Law School?
W That's true.

CA   Could I just quickly run through your qualifications, Professor. You hold a Bachelor of Arts from the University of Queensland?
W Yes.
CA A Bachelor of Laws with Honours also from the University of Queensland?
W Yes.
CA A Master of Laws from the University College of London?
W That's right.
CA A Graduate Certificate in Higher Education from Griffith University?
W Yes.
CA And also a Doctor of Philosophy from Griffith University?
W That's true.
CA   You describe, I think, your area of special interests as the law of politics.
W Yes.
CA Could you explain what you mean by that?
W The institutions, norms and black-letter law that regulate electoral democracy in particular, everything from parliamentary law in the old sense through – I've written quite a few books on election law, proper political parties, money in politics.

(Counsel Assisting, Mr Rice, seemed to know what 'black-letter law' meant. I needed to look it up. The Legal Dictionary within the Free Dictionary says it is 'a term used to describe basic principles of law that are accepted by a majority of judges in most states.')

CA The invitation, I think, perhaps prompted you to review the Local Government Electoral Act?

W Yes. I'm actually also writing a chapter on local government electoral law for a second edition of a book, so I'll put a plug in there. Yes, I had previously read some of the CMC material that led up to changes in the nature of groups, and I refreshed my mind about those things.

(The Crime and Misconduct Committee was the predecessor of the Crime and Corruption Committee.)

CA One topic of interest, I think you know, of this inquiry is on the operation of the provisions of the Act pertaining to groups. You have looked at the definition, I think, that's provided in the Local Government Electoral Act, and do you have a view about it?

W The definition is obviously broad and vague, and my submission, the gist of it, is that maybe we could consider focusing on the idea of what is an independent, because obviously running as an independent, and then thinking of, I guess, regulating the yin rather than the yang.

CA You mention that campaigning as an independent had a certain cachet. I think you used a different expression in your submission, that it was an electoral virtue?

W There is this sense that in local government, in particular, to be demarked as an independent has a cachet. That comes, I think, local government being the smaller bodies closer to the people.

But there's also political parties being on the nose. There has always been cynicism about that, but I think in the last decade or so there has been a rise in that kind of cynicism.

But counterweighted to that, as I say in my submission, is the fact that these are very large, complex bodies and it's almost unreasonable to imagine that they would ever be run without some kind of factions, groups, and it may be that we are in a transition phase where these councils one day will end up like the Brisbane City Council, with mature political parties, and I don't think that is a bad thing necessarily, because political parties provide a certain amount of stability.

CA The classification "independent" is one that is not actually used in the Local Government Act. Do you think that there should be some classification, with attributes that people could identify with, expressed within the legislation?

W Right. Well, it's quite common. In England and Wales, you can have a ballot label "independent".

CA So you are saying other jurisdictions –

W Other jurisdictions.

CA – do use that classification in a formal sense?

W Yes, the Act says that you can nominate yourself as an independent. Those other jurisdictions are not completely comparable, though, because in England and Wales local government has long been partisan.

I guess what I'm saying is that the incentive would be that you nominate as an independent and you get the virtue of the ballot label, which is a significant thing, especially in local government politics in larger jurisdictions where people may not have the same kinds of connections to candidates as they will have in smaller towns.

Unlike in the countries I have mentioned, the Act might then set out a series of things that, if independents do, they would be committing an offence and would possibly be ousted by the Court of Disputed Returns if they were elected.

(The problem I see is if everyone wanted to be an independent, the ballot paper would look a trifle silly. As Professor Orr says, this system works well in places where there are a substantial number of groups to contrast with independents.)

CA One view that has been expressed is that candidates could be required to compile a register of interests, which include affiliations, memberships and so forth, and then leave it to the public to judge the person's independence against those declarations of interest. Would you regard that as satisfactory?

W Right, so this would be a kind of statement that then gets published on a web?

CA Yes, or perhaps through the Electoral Commission or through some mechanism.

W Yes, okay. In many parts of Australia, in recent years, local governments have moved down that path, which is a bit like in trade union, corporate, even student elections, where there is some information beyond your name that is officially published, and that kind of disclosure might have some use.

I'm not sure if it gets at the heart of the problem that the Commission has been grappling with about these fuzzy entities of electoral groups, undeclared electoral groups, though, because I'm not sure what you would be required to do on this form. It's a bit like if you need a visa to get into the United States, you have to list every school you have ever gone to, every organisation you have ever donated money to.
CA And declare you are not a terrorist, among other things?
W Amongst other things, whether you've been involved in nuclear weapons, and so on. I have to declare that my brother is a nuclear physicist in France, and all these things. Really, that is not for gathering information. That procedure is designed that if you forget to put something in that list, they will be able to kick you out of the country on a technicality if they think you're a risk.

So it may be a good thing to give voters extra information, especially in some of these larger councils where they're not run by parties, but they're not word-of-mouth small towns.

(Unfortunately most of the incumbents urging disclosure of political and other affiliations seem to see it as liability for new candidates. 'We have to do it through the interests register; they should too' does not put a positive spin on the idea.

Also, we have Professor Orr's point that copious information gathering is used in the United States to expedite the deportation of citizens. 'You forgot to include your three years as a child in the Girl Guides so we're kicking you out as a possible terrorist.'

An analogy in Queensland of using information not for its expressed purpose might be if a candidate or a journalist used another candidate's association with a union against them. It sounds far-fetched, I say ruefully, but it can happen.)

CA One subject you touch on in your submission is the experience in other jurisdictions of the use of an agent. Perhaps you could explain what you are referring to by reference to an agent and what utility an agent might have in the electoral process?

W Okay. A potted history of all this is in the great war on electoral corruption in Britain and other Commonwealth countries in the 19th century, a significant moment in the late Victorian era was expenditure limits on candidates at local and parliamentary level.

CA It goes back to the 19th century?

W Yes, the Corrupt Practices Prevention Acts, and this involved the courts, it involved parliaments, it involved the culture and so on. One thing they did was that every candidate, at whatever level, had to nominate an agent, and that agent was then held to be strictly liable for anything that went wrong legally on the campaign. Now, that led in English law to a very strict and important position known as the electoral agent, which many lawyers, accountants and so on made quite a bit of money out of. I don't think we have that strict agency law in Queensland.

CA A lot wouldn't have the resources to engage such a person?

W Yes, and we don't have a business or a consultancy business, really, in Australia for lots of people who could be agents. We have people associated with political parties who could do it to help their political parties and so on, but we don't have that.

CA I suppose ideally, if that system works, then there will be stricter compliance with regulatory requirements?

W Ideally, yes.

CA Is that agency system in application at local government level in the UK?

W Yes.

CA Still, to your knowledge?

W To my knowledge. But it's also the case in the UK that local government is quite partisan, that people will still run – in fact, they have 300-plus registered parties, many of which are local organisations, so they don't seem to have the same cachet of running as an independent.

CA You have referred at the end of your submission to the desirability of education for candidates and politicians. Do you want to elaborate on what you have in mind that that education might consist of and how it might be provided?

W Okay. I'm highly conscious that we don't have – you can't just go and hire an election agent. It is not like the US, where there's a lot more literature and consultants out there that you can consult, assuming that you have the money, as a political activist or candidate. I've been working and over 20-odd years writing about it and talking to people, and people ring me up out of the blue wanting some help.

(In 2015, I rang Professor Orr out of the blue wanting some help.)

W Whilst as lawyers and academics we sometimes like there to be more law, because we feel like we're solving problems or it gives us more interesting work to do, we also have to be cognisant of the fact that local government, especially, involves thousands of people around the state, particularly in councils, that are part time, who you can – not over-regulate – you can create a sticky net in which sometimes the people most likely to be caught will be those who are just inadvertently innocent, whereas those who are well educated or have good lawyers to consult may find ways to avoid the law. –

We do need to ensure that some of these complex rules about campaign finance that have been building up for two decades now in Australia are better put in the public domain. Without criticising Electoral Commissions, because they're not all that highly resourced, I think that generally, in law, in the public service, we don't do a great job of explaining in simple, plain English the gist of the law.

I can understand also why Electoral Commissions might feel that they just should be pointing people to the law, because they can't be legal advisors. They don't want to have people saying, "You misled me about what the law was."

(Does the Law itself need reform so it is rendered in plain English? Can we have precision without painful expression? Public servants would feel more confident in providing information on laws if they were not so convoluted and cross-referential.)

CA Are you talking about plain English training?

W Yes, but I think if you look in some instances at – they're not perfect, but what the UK Election Commission has done, and they don't have to run their elections, so they have lots of resources to deal with campaign finance, candidate advice sessions and so on, but I think you can find – I have pulled off some examples here – guidance for candidates and agents that use the sorts of things that we have been saying for years to educators, have break-out boxes, use plain English.

- Have a break-out box
- Use plain English
- Read Bernie's book

CA. What role do you think timely disclosure of election funding has in the context of a system of private funding of non-endorsed candidates?

W It's crucial that we have timely disclosure. I've written in current affairs essays to promote that idea, having spent a little time in New York and spent a day at the New York Commission. For twenty years, the Big Apple is a huge electoral council, local government system, and they from the 1990s developed online disclosure in real time.

CA Could you give us the benefit of that experience? You are familiar with New York being perhaps one of the biggest cities.

W Yes, and one that had significant issues with corruption. It's not perfect, but they probably have the most highly developed –

CA What was the New York experience, if you don't mind, if you are able to assist us with that, with disclosure?

W Yes. Money, in a city like that where – remember, New York City Council helps run universities, hospitals. I mean, it's not like our city councils that are more service providers. So there's a lot at stake, a lot of history of corruption. There's an inability, because of the First Amendment, to outright cap electoral expenditure. New York moved down the path of sticks and carrots, so public funding, you opt in to expenditure limits, but also since the 1990s a system of real-time disclosure, which is significantly enforced, and New York has a very vibrant media.

What we're doing in Queensland with real-time disclosure I think has great potential, hopefully, in the local government sphere, particularly given how active local newspapers and radio journalists are. That's the case of we have to wait and see and suck it and see, but I don't think disclosure on its own is a cure for anything.

(Especially when the Queensland real-time disclosure laws were found wanting in their first test at the Ipswich by-election.)

CA Just getting back to the New York experience, you mentioned that the real-time disclosure was enforced?

W They do their very best.

CA What kind of mechanism is there for enforcement? Is it scrutiny by the media and public or something of a more regulatory kind?

W A more regulatory kind. In America, electoral and other authorities see themselves more as regulators than administrators. Again, without criticising the Commissions, I think we are coming out of a more traditional model, public service model.

CA There's a lot of emphasis on trust, it seems?

W Yes, and particularly outside parliamentary elections, where you have 100 local government areas. New York City has a significantly resourced city election commission, boards, courts – a lot of enforcement going on.

CA Including prosecutions?

W Yes. Oh, yes, including during campaigns, of high-profile figures and their associates. Personally, that cat-and-mouse game of disclosure/enforcement only gets you so far.

CA Why do you say that?

W My submission I think might touch on this. I think there are other issues about – when we are thinking about campaign finance, we can't just think about an ideal integrity model. It's important, but free and fair elections involve questions of relative equality of arms, and that's why in other jurisdictions they focus on expenditure limits, and that has been the history in Britain for a long time, or capping donations.

CA You have told us that capping on funding in fact goes back to the 19th century –

W Yes.

CA – and is still applied in other jurisdictions around the world?

W Yes.

CA The justification, I suppose, is reduction or levelling the playing field, is that one justification?

W Yes, one justification is the political equality one. Another one, at least initially, was to take some of the heat out of campaigns because of all the bribery and so on that was going on in the 19th century.

CA Do you have a feel, then, for how successful capping is to achieve those objectives?

W Even that involves two questions. One is what do you include in expenditure? How well do you enforce it? So there are practical questions. But at the moment, we see there are a dozen or more conservative politicians who are being caught up in the net of not fully disclosing, going over the limits of their expenditure, their agents making mistakes in the law and so on. The degree to which it translates into local politics – I would have thought if the ideal of local politics is encouraging all sorts of citizens to be able to stand, then there is a very good argument to say expenditure limits.

(Expenditure caps are not such a big issue at local government level. Most campaigns are self-funded, apart from donations from family and friends, in most cases, totalling a few hundred dollars.

It would be difficult to argue against the $100,000, $200,000 and $300,000 spent on mayoral elections by successful candidates in south-east Queensland which has huge councils over considerable areas. It is not that the winners are spending too much; it is the losers have far too little to spend.

It might be capped, say, at $100,000 for mayors and $10,000 for other councillors. For an average Australian wage earner, $10,000 is a lot of money and spending $100,000 is impossible.

The issues we need to be discussing in-depth are not expenditure caps, worthy as they are, but public funding of candidates, providing cost-effective free communications during campaigns, and even de-amalgamation of large councils.)

CA You have written in favour, have you not, of capping of expenditure and donations – or at least in favour of the Queensland laws before they were repealed?

W Of the intent behind them.

CA The intent, okay.

W The devil is always in the detail. At what level do you appoint these limits? I have also written critically about public funding. That can become a bit of an incumbency rort, obviously. I particularly think expenditure limits have a value that capping donations doesn't have, at least in terms of enforcement. Donations happen in private. If not, we wouldn't need disclosure laws.

(Public funding, at the State and Federal Government level might be an incumbency rort for the Labor, Liberal and National parties. But, at the local government level, lack of public finding assists sitting councillors and mayors who have access to donors. One of the reasons incumbents get re-elected is they greatly outspend new candidates, campaigning on peanuts.

I support public funding of local government candidates as I do not see expenditure caps doing much to even up the playing field. Most candidates will not have resources near the cap. You would imagine the caps would be considered adequate amounts for running an effective campaign. In that case, nearly every candidate cannot afford to run an effective campaign. That to me signals a problem.

As an example, we can look at the total of donations above $200 to mayoral candidates at the 2016 Moreton Bay Regional Council election. Here they are from least to most donated:

- Barry Bolton $0
- James McNaught $0
- Jason Woodforth $0
- Shayne Hogan $500
- Dean Teasdale $990
- Allan Sutherland $188,087.05.)

CA Do you think there is a utility in exploring, for the sake of reducing corruption levels or the

perception of it and levelling the playing field, exploring the idea of caps at local government level?
W Yes, because for a variety of reasons, political equality may be taking some of the heat out of the system. People are saying, look, I don't want to necessarily be part of this, many, many hundreds of thousands of dollars on campaigns. Also there is a lot of cynicism about excessive advertising and so on. People crave more creative forms of campaigning that might at least appear to be more direct. You can do things on the internet and social media now that cost less, that engage people possibly more.

Certainly doorknocking and traditional campaigning is something that studies have shown the average voter values, and I think we particularly value at local government level, given the old saying that local government is meant to be closer to the people. So I think for a variety of reasons, yes, expenditure limits need to be considered.
CA Thanks, Professor.
W You're welcome.

23

TRANSPARENCY IS A GREAT CIVIC VIRTUE and it is worthwhile to ponder why. A reliable ethical test for a councillor's intended action is 'would I like to see what I am about to do on the front page of the *Black Stump Bugle?*'

Some politicians and media have taken to judging an action by whether it passes the pub test. I would rather ask whether it passes the publicity test, the wisdom of the readership of the *Black Stump Bugle*, which goes by the acronym BSB and is as legendary in rural Australia as the Bachelor and Spinsters Ball. (I would warn the gullible I am making most of this stuff up, but the allegory is sound.)

It was at one such B & S ball, sponsored by the *Black Stump Bugle*, where the concept of the wisdom of the readership was spawned. The ball fund-raising contest, at a halfpenny a guess, involved estimating the number of hard boiled lollies in a large jar.

The local book-keeper, Francis Galton, was the auditor of the contest. He noted the median guess of 1207 lollies was accurate within 1 per cent of the true count of 1198 sweets. You can bet on the collective intuition of the crowd.

Six councillors accepting mayoral candidate Allan Sutherland's largesse in paying for co-starring roles on advertising billboards, in my not-so-humble opinion, offends the wisdom of the readership.

Two of the six were Labor Party members, Koliana Winchester and Mick Gillam. Allan Sutherland stood against Labor twice in state elections in the 1990s. He severed party ties many years ago but he publicly supported the opponent of Labor candidate Yvette D'Ath in the 2014 state by-election for Redcliffe. In my not-so-humble opinion, Cr Sutherland's much vaunted independence might have been exemplified by his offering no comment on that state election. Ms D'Ath is now state Attorney-General.

(Cr Gillam told me Allan Sutherland suggested he donate his share of the billboard cost to a local charity which Cr Gillam said he subsequently did.)

Considerations aside of muddied waters where independence meets party allegiance, was it appropriate for a mayoral candidate to offer to contribute to the campaign expenses of candidates whom he would be most likely serving alongside? The wise readership of the Back Stump Bugle cites the principle of 'who pays the piper calls the tune' and says the answer is 'no, it was not appropriate'. Was it appropriate for the six councillors to accept the mayor's offer? No, says the wise Bugle readership, it was inappropriate. I will add my opinion to that of the readership and say the six should not have done it.

A motorist driving along Gympie Rd, might have spied the billboard with the visages of Candidates Allan Sutherland, Mike Charlton, and Mick Gillam.

That driver might think that each of the three believed the other two were doing good work on Council. Give the driver the knowledge that Allan Sutherland paid the full cost of the billboard with money donated by Moreton Futures Trust. Chances are the driver's new perception is not as benign the earlier one.

I do concede many motorists might have said, 'I've seen those blokes around somewhere; I might vote for them' which ties the value of billboard advertising to the value of incumbency.

Some years ago, I had a personal experience of the practice of the principle of 'who pays the piper calls the tune'. I was on a community panel helping to derive the arts support strategy of Moreton Bay Council at a day-long workshop. Having dabbled in social-science research at university, I was surprised how complimentary of council the discussion topics, surveys, and presentation at the end of the day were. I realised if you are a consultant and you want another council gig, it pays to play nice.

On another occasion Moreton Bay Council paid a consultancy to provide a range of options for an expensive project. The consultants came up with a dozen options and recommended one. Council powerbrokers did not like that option and commissioned another consultant with a narrower brief, to prepare the case for the option they did like.

As much as councillors vaunt their independence, outside independent forthright analysis on council matters is not always well received. For many years,

I was a council reporter, as well as doing general reporting for the *Pine Rivers Press* and *Northern Times* newspapers. I was in both roles at the time of the inaugural 2008 Moreton Council election. After the election, I prepared a front-page story on the donors to and beneficiaries of the trust, Advancing Moreton Leadership. Before a Council meeting, one councillor said loudly to me and within hearing of the other councillors, including those named in the story, 'I hope you never put me on the front page of the Pine Rivers Press.' I was chuffed at that remark because normally a Councillor would give a kidney to be on the front page.

One editor subsequently removed me from Council reporting without explanation. I approached him about it but all he would say was, 'That's my decision.'

Over the years I watched a series of junior reporters sacrificed to the flattery, bonhomie, and off-the-record goss of cunning councillors.

Of course, I still wrote council stories, for the editor to water down. I had a standard structure in my stories where I would put the case of a resident or residents on a council issue and at the bottom of the story I would put the council rebuttal. Only the editor would often move the rebuttal to the top of the story which in effect said, 'nothing to read here'. The editor had quite a comical approach to story-telling, in an absurdist kind of way.

24

'POLITICS MAKES STRANGE BEDFELLOWS' was an observation which evolved in the nineteenth century, adapted from a line in Shakespeare's *The Tempest*. It first appeared in print in *My Summer in a Garden*, a book by Charles Dudley Warner. The way Warner weaved the saying into a sentence, it may well have been a plump fruit of folk wisdom. Almost 200 years later the lack of politics in council elections also makes strange bedfellows.

Jim Soorley is a former Labor Lord Mayor of Brisbane and was a prominent member of Logan Futures, a third party company which raised $377,000 to elect Cr Luke Smith as mayor of Logan City in 2016. Cr Smith, in 2010, was the unsuccessful LNP candidate for the Federal seat of Rankin. His main opponent for 2016 mayor in Logan was Brett Raguse, like Soorley, a Labor Party member. Raguse held the traditionally conservative Federal seat of Forde for one term from 2007.

Labor governments made Mr Soorley chair of Unitywater and CS Energy – a state-owned electricity generator.

Unitywater supplies water and sewerage to residents of Moreton Bay Regional Council, Noosa, and Sunshine Coast Councils. The councils own Unitywater but they like to call themselves shareholders of the water dispenser. They say Unitywater is independent. Unitywater has delivered savage increases in the price of water since its formation in 2010. In its 2010-11 report, Unitywater defensively stated its public complaints were running at fewer than 10 in a thousand. Suffice to say, in Moreton Bay Region, Unitywater is about as popular as Lady Macbeth on Mother's Day.

His chair of CS Energy makes Soorley a coal baron of sorts as CS owns three coal fired power stations – Kogan, Callide, and Gladstone. To show he cannot get enough of being on the wrong side of energy history, Mr Soorley in 2017 joined the board of TerraCom, which bought the Blair Athol coal mine in Central Queensland.

The former Roman Catholic priest obviously believes idle hands are the Devil's workshop as he is also the chair of the LGAQ and its service organisation Propel, which sold long-term contracts to Liverpool and Ipswich councils when Carl Wulff was CEO at each one. Ipswich is an historic coal-mining town. Mr Soorley seems to have an affinity for the black nuggets of power. Who knows? The obsession might have a psychological dimension similar to that of the protagonist in the classic film *Citizen Kane*. Maybe Mr Soorley was deprived of a toy steam train as a child. *Choo train* could be Mr Soorley's *Rosebud*.

Ironically Mr Soorley, in office as Brisbane Lord Mayor, was known for run-ins with Labor Premiers Wayne Goss and Peter Beattie. His more recent relations with State Labor Governments and one LNP Government have been more benign.

In December 2017, CCC officers executed a search warrant for the offices of Logan City Council.

Transcript #13
Abridged by Bernie Dowling

Witness Luke Smith, June 13, 2017
PO, Presiding Officer Alan MacSporran QC
CA, Counsel Assisting, Glen Rice QC
W, Luke Smith

CA Is your name Timothy Luke Smith?
W Yes, it is.
CA Mr Smith, you are Logan City Mayor; is that right?
W That's correct.
CA Councillor, you successfully contested the mayoral election in Logan in 2016; is that correct?
W That's correct.
CA You have something of a Liberal National Party background; am I right?
W I was in the LNP for, I think, three years, by memory.
CA You also contested a federal election, I think?
W That's correct, yes.
CA Not successful on that occasion?
W I was not successful, no, for the federal election.
CA But you were running as a Liberal National Party candidate?

W That's correct.

CA When did you decide that you would be a (mayoral) candidate?

W Roughly around the same time that Mayor (Pam) Parker made her announcement that she was going to not contest the next election.

(Ms Parker made the announcement on March 6, 2015. She said she was not going to endorse a successor. Ms Parker kept her resolve for 12 months before declaring support for Luke Smith in early March, 2016. A newspaper poll accompanying the story of the Parker patronage attracted more than 2100 respondents saying whom they would vote for. More than 55 per cent answered Brett Raguse and about 23 per cent preferred the ultimate winner Luke Smith.)

CA You did, in the end, raise a very large amount; am I right?

W That's correct.

CA I think, according to one of the disclosure returns, it's in the order of $377,000?

W That's correct.

CA What were the means of raising that? There were donations, I think, from donors?

W Yes, there were donations. We had a couple of fundraising events, golf days, dinners, and events like that where people had opportunity to donate.

CA Can I show you this document?

W Thank you.

CA Is that a set of minutes for a meeting of a campaign executive group dated 22 April 2015?

W Yes, they're certainly called minutes.

CA They reflect, don't they, a mayoral campaign executive meeting, as the title suggests?

W That's correct.

CA The group that was gathered for that meeting included you and your wife. We see the list of attendees there. Could you perhaps tell us in what capacity the others attended?

W Sure. Would you like me to go through the names individually?

CA Yes, please.

W Jim Soorley has been a mentor of mine since 2008 and has also had experience in running campaigns.

CA We see from the minutes that the very first item involved discussion about the establishment of a shelf company for fundraising activities?

W That's correct.

CA Why was that desirable?

W I'd spent some time with the Electoral Commission to try and understand the best way to handle a large amount of funds. We recognised that we would need roughly between $350,000 to $400,000 to run a very decent and professional campaign, given that it was my first campaign as Mayor. I wanted it to be open and transparent through a Pty Ltd company.

CA We see on page 4, towards the middle of the page, another suggestion that came up. Do you see in that paragraph that's displayed, commencing "JS advised", there was discussion about suppliers to

Logan City Council. The minutes record you as having been hesitant to approach companies, being a reference, I think you would agree, to suppliers to the Logan City Council. What was the source of your reluctance to approach suppliers to the council?

W Oh, I just found that as a conflict. I'm not – there's no-one on my – who donated to me that are suppliers to Logan City Council.

CA No, but there was discussion about whether that was one means of attracting money, gaining money?

W At this meeting, yes, there was that discussion.

CA That suppliers to the council might be approached for the purpose of getting donations for your campaign?

W That is reflected in the minutes, yes.

CA The minutes record your being hesitant about that, and in response to that, Mr Soorley, it seems, according to the minutes, suggested that the approach would be through third parties, and not from you, and that that would be a satisfactory response to your hesitance. Was that the discussion?

W I don't recall the conversation, but I can say very clearly that there are no suppliers who donated to my campaign.

CA I understand that. I am just questioning you about your approach to fundraising as at this time.

W Okay.

CA That was a live proposal, wasn't it, that you or someone on your behalf, perhaps Mr Soorley, might approach suppliers for Logan City Council?

W I believe that's what you're seeing in the minutes.

CA Yes.

W I don't recall the conversation off the top of my head.

CA Okay. You don't recall some discussion of that kind which is set out in fairly specific detail in the minutes – you don't recall that occurring?

W No, I don't believe it did occur, no.

CA You don't believe it did occur?

W No.

CA You think the minutes –

W Sorry, sorry. I believe the discussion occurred. I apologise. I don't believe the actual action happened.

CA Two different things; I accept that.

W Yes.

CA It's clear, isn't it, that the subject of discussion was that suppliers to the council would be approached or could be approached by third parties, such as Mr Soorley, to attract donations from that source?

W I accept that's what the minutes reflect.

CA In approaching a supplier of goods or services to the council for a donation, would such an approach not carry with it the implication that if the supplier didn't donate, the supplier might in future not be a supplier to the council?

W I think my integrity inside my operation as Mayor and Councillor is not in question here, and I don't accept that, no.

(It might well be the CCC is questioning Mr Smith's perceived integrity. Their October report read, 'Operation Belcarra focused on five allegations in relation to the 2016 local government election in Logan.

These allegations involved perceptions that Cr Luke Smith, Mayor of the Logan City Council (LCC) had failed to give a disclosure return within the required time or provided a disclosure return containing information that he knew was false or misleading, and had attempted to unlawfully influence council decisions relating to his donors. At the time of writing this report, these allegations were still being finalised by the CCC.'

Obviously, the last of the allegations is the most serious. Mr Smith declined an invitation from a fellow councillor to resign as Mayor. He submitted a reply to the CCC report but that reply does not appear on the Logan City Council website.

CCC Chairman Alan MacSporran had the Operation Belcarra report tabled in State Parliament on October 4, 2017, with the broad remark, 'A number of matters remain under active investigation by the CCC.')

CA Did you agree, though – notwithstanding the hesitance that you have described, did you agree, as the minutes record, to compile a list of suppliers for the purpose of being approached?

W I never actually followed through with that action.

CA Did you agree to compile such a list, as the minute records?

W At the meeting, I guess I did. I can't remember, but that's actually what the minutes say.

CA To be clear, you say you didn't follow through with that?

W That's correct.

CA Did you compile any list of that kind?

W I can't remember.

CA We see in the second entry in that box a related task. Can I suggest that the task attributed to Mr Soorley was to contact the donors as referred to in the list above, which is referable to you? In other words, you do the list, and then he'll do the contacting. That's how the minutes record it?

W That's what the minutes say, that's correct.

25

COMEDIAN ROBIN WILLIAMS had a great joke about cocaine being God's way of saying you've got too much money. Developers are God's way of saying a community has too much money.

Shelter is a human need and a human right. But building a dwelling involves a conquest and killing of the fauna and flora previously living on the land you erect your building on. From my experience such considerations are not on the radar of most developers. You've gotta watch them if you are a friend of the environment.

Developers are primarily concerned with building shelters, as many as they can on the land they acquired as cheaply as they could. You've gotta watch them in case they are tempted to gain permission to cram dwellings onto marginally liveable land such as that subject to flooding or considered dangerous to build on, such as acid-sulphate soil, or land near precious waterways or liable to the ravages of future climate change

Town planning laws are the institutionalised way of watching developers. Unfortunately some of the interpreters of those laws, town planners, are in the pocket of developers so you have to watch them, too.

Councils derive most of their incomes from rates which means those with land able to support dwellings will tend to be pro-development. You have to watch them, too.

Economist Dr Cameron Murray has come up with a plan which increases the income of councils and reduces the wealth and hopefully influence of developers.

Transcript #14
Abridged by Bernie Dowling

Witness Dr Cameron Murray, April 28, 2017
PO, Presiding Officer Alan MacSporran QC
CA, Counsel Assisting, Glen Rice QC
W, Cameron Murray

CA I call Dr Cameron Murray.
PO Dr Murray, do you have any objection to taking an oath on the Bible?
W..No.
PO Thank you.
W..The evidence which I shall give in these proceedings shall be the truth, the whole truth, and nothing but the truth. So help me God.
CA Is your name Cameron Keith Murray?
W..Correct.
CA You're an economist, I think, Dr Murray?
W..Correct.
CA You work at – which university, just remind me?
W..University of Queensland.

CA   You have a range of qualifications, I think, commencing with a Bachelor of Applied Science, with a major in property economics, from QUT?
W..Correct, yes.
CA Master of Business Research and Environmental Economics from QUT?
W..That's right.
CA   And also a Doctor of Philosophy, majoring in economics, from the University of Queensland?
W..That's right.

   (We've established you're a brainy bloke, Dr Murray.)
CA You're appearing, I think, in response to a notice to attend today?
W..That's right.
CA Can I show you this.
W..Sure thing.
CA Is that a copy of your attendance notice?
W..To the best of my knowledge.
CA I tender that.
PO Exhibit 100.
CA You responded to an invitation from the CCC and made a submission to this inquiry?
W..That's right.
CA I'll just ask you to confirm this, if you wouldn't mind.
W..Not a problem.
CA Is that a copy of your submission, Dr Murray?
W..It looks like it to me.
CA I tender that.
PO Exhibit 101.

CA You have a special interest, I think, in areas of corruption, property development, property markets?

W..Correct.

CA And environmental economics?

W..That's right.

CA Could I just ask you to flesh out some features of your submission?

W Sure thing.

CA In the local government area, by virtue of the fact that candidates, by and large, are not party endorsed, there is a private funding model.

W..Mmm-hmm.

CA So that candidates either fund themselves or obtain funding by way of donations from some other source.

W..That's right.

CA You have commented, I think, on the disadvantages of that model?

W..I guess I've commented on the fact that not knowing the sources of those donations is a problem, but in principle it's not a problem. But the system could be improved to have some public donations, so that there is a more competitive field of potential candidates rather than those who are likely to succeed by attracting the most donations and simply reinforcing their success. So there's certainly scope to improve the system and add a public funding element, but per se private funding – you know, it's not such a bad thing.

CA If there was a component of public funding, would you favour the continuation of a proportion of private funding, and to what extent?

W..I actually think that whatever rule you come up with about private funding is going to have very little effect. Even if you pick a number and say it's $50,000, I think that the advantages that would have gone via formal donations will come via other means, so that a cap itself will have very little practical effect on those seeking favour using donations. They'll find other means instead.

CA It's capable of being circumvented; is that what you're referring to?

W..That's what I am suggesting, that a cap on private donations will be circumvented. And we've seen caps on donations in other jurisdictions being avoided by other sorts of gift-giving and informal agreements.

CA So are you not in favour, by virtue of that, of capping of donations?

W..I'm in favour if there's a legitimate enforcement mechanism and monitoring, but I think what we've seen is that getting that sort of mechanism and monitoring and that institutional set-up correct is very, very difficult.

(I think it could be more a question of lack of will rather than being able to effectively allocate resources.)

W I would like to have a go at it, but I don't think it's going to be a great solution to the problem we're facing of seeking influence of councillors. It may put some sand in the gears and make it a little bit more difficult to carry out.

CA Would you regard the banning of donations as being realistic, as opposed to capping?

W..I think there is a way – it's possible if the political will was there and the investment was made to enforce that sort of thing, that it would be fine, but I think that would be circumvented as well through private gift-giving, other sorts of indirect favouritism and appointments to token jobs, that sort of thing, which are just a way to funnel cash. There will be many, many alternative ways to get around that.

But if you want to do it, as I said, anything you do to put sand in the gears of favouritism, I would support.

CA There are certain vehicles of donation that you have submitted against, including donations from trusts being an intermediary between a donor and a recipient?

W Correct.

CA Why do you take that position?

W..I think if we care about political accountability, we have to have some lens through which to see who is being influenced and how, and trusts are just a way to hide where the money is coming from.

I actually spent four years researching the political connections of landowners in Queensland. I looked at 12,000 different landowners. I had 163,000 relationships in my network, from corporate relationships, cross-directorships on boards of directors, and the thing that held me up was when a trust owned the land and I couldn't find out who was behind it or when a trust donated, and that's where I got stuck. So anyone seeking to investigate things, it's just a dead end.

That's why I think it either should be banned, or we could even look further about the nature of trust structures themselves.

(While I have enormous suspicions of trust, I would prefer better regulation to a ban.)

CA What was the purpose of the research of which you spoke?

W..The research I did as part of my PhD looked at whether I could predict favourable land rezoning from political donations or relationship networks of the landowners, taking the view that where the boundary was drawn on the map is a decision about who wins a windfall gain on one side of that line and got rezoned and who loses.

Now, if it was a characteristic of the land, we should see that the land would be somewhat different, different in size, something like that, because all my land was next door or across the road. But in fact what I found was that you can predict where the boundary gets drawn by the relationship network of the landowner, how well connected they are to what I would call the corporate and political network in Queensland, those who are on boards of companies together, those who have worked in companies that – in my case, it was the ULDA that did the land rezoning, a state body. Those landowners where employees of the ULDA had worked for them before – that was a good predictor. Those who employed professional lobbyists – in my data, the professional lobbyists had a 100 per cent success rate in making sure your land got rezoned instead of just missing out.

What the previous witness we had here said is correct: political donations did not predict who got favoured, and that was partly because everyone was donating to both sides of politics. There was just an abundance of donations at the state level, and I couldn't pick apart whether that donation was leading to that favour, because there were plenty of donations they gave that didn't lead to the favour.

So in my view, it's not really the donations, but it's everything else that goes alongside them, all those alternatives to donations – the professional lobbyists, hiring former politicians to sit on your board as in-house lobbyists. I mean, the list is as long as my arm of former politicians in Queensland who work for property developers internally. They get to avoid being on the lobbyist register, because you have to be a professional lobbyist to be on the register, yet they can leave politics on Friday and work for – I know Campbell Newman works for Springfield Land Corporation, one of your witnesses is a 25 per cent owner of them, the next day.

Of course, nothing we're talking about today is going to stop that, but that's where the real influence comes from.

CA Not from donations?

W..Donations – I've actually done a lot of other research on donations, about who's donating, what proportions they give to what political party and at what time, not so much at the local level but at the state and federal level. What you find in Australia is 60 per cent of the donation value comes from donors who donate equally to both parties. So they're not about getting the person who's aligned with them politically into power. They're about signalling to whoever gets into power, "If you do me a favour, my credit's good and I'll sort you out later." So donations are just one way to start this chain of reciprocity going.

(But at local level without political parties and with incumbents likely to be returned donations are potentially more effective.)

W There are plenty of examples I've looked at in Queensland. One is Flinders, which is a land development in Logan City Council. In that situation, the landowner didn't donate a cent. Instead, they would drive the councillors around. "What would you like to see here? What would you like to see here? Come to my meeting. Come to my vision meeting, where I'll employ planners to tell you what we can build here, these grand visions."

They employed professional lobbyists, and they got their land rezoned. They did everything but donations. So whatever rules we change as a result of this inquiry would have had absolutely zero effect, and I estimate that they got a gain of around $80 million to $100 million from a planning decision after doing that.

CA Do I sum it up correctly, you consider that networking and lobbying have far more leverage than donations?

W..Correct.

CA Although donations, I think you have said, have their place in establishing a relationship of reciprocity?

W..Correct. My research suggests that donations are more like a ticket to entry for newcomers to this relationship network. So if you're not already at the table and well entrenched, then you need to work your way towards the centre, and so you would want to donate. What we see in the donations data is that the largest donors these days are, for example, new Chinese developers. They're donating the most, because they're not at the table. They're not in the network. They have to buy their way in. One of the former witnesses here said we should ban developer donations. That would suit him perfectly because he has already got a seat at the table. He's already right in the middle of the network. That stops any new kids on the block coming to enter the network and compete for the political favours.

(But if you take the long view on banning donations, once developers leave the table, other developers will not be able to buy a replacement seat. Think of it like a nightclub queue where entry used to be bought when someone left the club. Only now, you still can't get in when someone leaves. Dr

Murray's point about delving further when a developer wants donations banned is instructive.)

CA You've raised an interesting matter in your submission by referring to what you call the value of council decisions.

W..Correct.

CA You make the point that valuable decisions are made by councils to confer benefits, effectively, for nothing?

W..Correct.

CA Would you like to explain that for us?

W.Sure. The reason we're here today and the reason New South Wales had an inquiry into rezoning and developer donations was because we've decided as a community that giving additional property rights to particular landowners should be done for free instead of at market prices.

CA You talk about zoning, for example?

W..Correct. So you can imagine that I own a plot of land and I can build a single-unit dwelling. Okay? When the rule changes so I can build a 10-storey building, that's a new property right that attaches to that land, that is owned by the community, that should be sold. Okay? And there are examples in Brazil where they auction additional rights to develop at high densities.

They're sold at market prices and landowners must compete with each other to bid for that, and they essentially sell it to them. In the ACT, they don't have auctions. Instead, they charge 75 per cent of the value gain as a tax. Okay? So it's essentially a sale at a 25 per cent discount. So if we had that sort of system, the pie that everybody is fighting over and that everybody is trying to work their networks and get those favours for would be much, much smaller. It would be 75 per cent smaller.

I've calculated that if we just adopted the ACT system, that's $1.7 billion across Queensland that could be raised that is, instead, given away to selected landowners for free.

CA   Just to develop that a little more so we understand the ACT model, upon rezoning –

W..No. Upon – sorry. Sorry to interrupt.

CA No, no, by all means.

W..You can do any zoning decision you like, draw any lines on any map, but when someone takes their land from its current use and seeks permission to change the use, so the equivalent in Queensland would be an application for a material change of use, the assessor of that checks if it's consistent with the plan and then says, "Well, your land at this new use is worth maybe $3 million. The land at the old use was worth $1 million. We'll send you a bill for 75 per cent of the difference and then stamp your approval."

CA How is the valuation undertaken?

W..It's internal valuers, very much like how annual land valuations are undertaken. They're done by valuers who defend their valuations in court.

CA All right, that's one model.

W..That's right.

CA What's the other model? You mentioned Brazil, I think.

W..That's right. So instead of drawing that line on the map and rezoning, you draw the line and say you can build to that additional density, but you must come and buy the additional right to get that additional density. So if you are a light industrial user and you want to develop, for example, here at New Farm or at West End or something like that, and you want to develop a 12-storey building, you come and buy that at our auctions, and we're going to auction the right.
CA Those suggestions would have an attraction in terms of raising revenue?
W..Correct.
CA Do they have an attraction in terms of limitation of corruption, or the perception of it?
W..Well, the attraction is that when the pie is radically shrunk, there's a lot less to go and nurture your relationships over. So rather than getting – for example, in the case of Flinders I talked about, Undullah is the suburb it's in – rather than $80 million or $100 million of value, it would only be $15 million or $20 million, that additional gain from the decision. So you would invest a lot less time for a $10 million or $15 million or $20 million pot in nurturing those relationships and hiring the lobbyists and jumping through all those hoops than you would for an $80 million or a $100 million pot.
CA You're in favour of that kind of a system, by the sound of it?
W..My general view is that when you have things of large private value that are given away with discretion through the political system, you should

do your best to charge market value for them. Otherwise, it's a bit like running a lottery and having it decided by a committee. Of course the relatives of that committee are always going to end up winning that lottery. But if we reduce that value down massively, we at least have less willingness to participate.

CA Are there any downsides, then, to levying some sort of tax or impost on decisions that affect land value?

W..The downside is that it's political suicide. There was one imposed in Sydney in the early 1970s. It lasted three years. It was a 30 per cent tax on the gain from rural to urban transition of land. Basically, all the wealthy landowners who wanted to bank on subdividing their land then mobilised their efforts to get rid of the government and make sure that that was squashed.

(This is a huge issue in Australia across a lot of commerce when the wealthy have the money to persuade voters their private interest coincides with the public good. It is the tapeworm eating away at the Benthamite principal of the greatest good for the greatest number.

Governments can try to financially counter the negative campaigns of vested interests but that erodes the profits from an equitable revenue-raising measure and success is not guaranteed. Often it is easier for a government to roll over and re-instate the old bad policy or severely water down the new one.)

W   I can tell you now, if you propose this in Queensland, I've interviewed former senior bureaucrats and people who have worked for politicians in Queensland, and they've told me that if you raise the words "betterment tax", which is what it's traditionally known as, in these circles, no-one will talk to you again. You will be shunned. It's a signal that you are not part of this group, this favoured group.

CA As a politician or councillor?

W..Correct. A politician, councillor, anyone who is already within those groups who realises that they're giving favours worth a lot of money to other people who are going to repay them with favours in the future, whether directly or indirectly, they will think it's bad and they'll believe that it's bad for some particular reason. These people are no different to you and me. They're just in a different social situation. They will believe it's bad and they won't want to do it, because it will upset their networks. It will upset their friends and family. So they will believe what they say. It must be bad.

If you proposed it, if the Queensland Government proposed it tomorrow, you would see a backlash from the property industry, the Stocklands, the Lend Leases. Bob Sharpless would surely be involved at funding a massive campaign to get rid of the government that proposed that. And of course it would be worth $1.7 billion a year to them to run that campaign, because that's what my calculation shows

Maaate!

is what's going to be given up, this $1.7 billion freebie.

CA   You point to some differences between Queensland and the ACT in terms of landholdings. But even allowing for that, how long has that system been in operation in the ACT?

W..The tax on the value gain?

CA Yes.

W Since 1971.

CA Has that resistance that you have spoken of from the property industry been evident there?

W..As I said, the political opportunity was ripe because the conversion of rural to urban uses in the ACT is only done by the ACT Government, because they only have leasehold rural land. In fact, all their land is leasehold. But for urban uses, it's 99 years. So there isn't a development lobby and there has never been a big development lobby in the ACT, purely because it constructed originally a system of land titles that prohibited land banking and speculation on changes of use, even from 1911 or whenever it was first implemented.

CA Thanks, Dr Murray.

W..That's all? Thank you.

PO Thanks, Dr Murray. Thanks for coming. You are excused.

W..Thank you.

PO Mr Rice, that's the only evidence today?

CA That's the last witness for the day and that's the last witness that's scheduled for this hearing. Commissioner, I am advised that the investigation of

Operation Belcarra remains ongoing and that consequent upon information provided by some witnesses, further inquiries are being undertaken, which could give rise to further witnesses giving evidence at another time. Accordingly, my submission is that it would be appropriate to adjourn the proceedings to a date to be fixed rather than finalising the hearing today.

PO Yes, thank you. I accept that. We'll adjourn, then, the inquiry to a date to be fixed.

26

MAYORAL CANDIDATE TOM TATE, who is used to driving a Ferrari, looked wobbly riding a BMX bike before the 2016 election. His cycling was for a cute photo op of Mr Tate riding the campaign trail.

Mr Tate said a council he led would help remove 30,000 cars from the Gold Coast streets during the 2018 Commonwealth Games being held there. You had the feeling his Ferrari would not be one of them. Me, I am a transport bigot. I won't vote for someone who owns a car worth more than a house in Southport. But that's just me and not the majority of Gold Coast Council voters in 2016.

Mr Tate does not need a bicycle nor a kale smoothie to be a hipster. He's a natural. On November 17, 2017, Cr Tate took fingers to Facebook – all right, it wasn't Instagram but give him a break, at least he's trying. He posted to congratulate Gold Coast singer, Amy Shark on her appearance on US television, show, *The Late Late Show with James Corden.*

The local paper described Shark as 'one of the Gold Coast's most successful musical acts' and the Corden show as a 'top rating US late night talk show'. Neither of these descriptions was accurate but parochialism comes before precision in the operations manual of some newspapers.

To be fair to the local News Corp paper, Fairfax's Sydney Morning Herald was impressed by Shark's 'performance on one of the country's top-rating late night shows'.

Here are the late-night numbers for November 13-17, 2017: 11.30pm: Jimmy Fallon .60, Stephen Colbert .47, Jimmy Kimmel .46; 12.30pm: Seth Meyers .35, James Corden .29. What was impressive but unreported by the Herald was Corden's 2017 musical guests included Green Day, Ed Sheeran, Harry Styles, Kings of Leon, Iggy Azalea, Macklemore, and Fergie.

Shark battled for many years for success in the music business before she scored a surprise second in the 2016 Triple J national radio Hottest-100 popularity contest with her single *Adore*.

This fostered a hook-up with producer M-Phazes, a recording contract, an extensive overseas tour, six ARIA nominations, global promotion by Apple Music, and Facebook lauding by Hipster Tate of Shark as a 'superstar'. Shark took home two ARIAs on November 28, 2017 – one for Breakthrough Artist and one for Best Pop Release.

Unlike Shark, Mr Tate did not have to struggle in his business. His father gave him the Islander Resort Hotel in Surfers Paradise to manage. Daddy left Thomas the fancy pub in his will. The family lineage was like that in the song *Copperhead Road*:

'Now Daddy ran the whiskey in a Surfers pub.
I sold it to a bookie; I'm on the up and up.'

In 2015, Cr Tate sold the pub to Brisbane nightclub owner and former bookmaker Lou Bickle for $26.5 million so unkind critics could not say the Mayor had a conflict of interest. (Instead the unkind harped about his inherited wealth. You just can't win with some people.) Cr Tate also says he funds his own election campaign. These acts of selflessness did not stop ABC Television's *Four Corners* program questioning, in September 2017, the Mayor's close ties to Gold Coast developers. The program went by the amusing if a trifle nasty title *All That Glitters*, a reference to the usually disparaging Gold Coast nickname of the Glitter Strip. The alternative moniker, the Goldie, sounds twee to me but some of the denizens and a lot of the tourists seem to like it. As far as I know, residents of the Sunshine Coast don't go around referring to their council area as the Sunnie.

Cr Tate is suing the ABC and his fellow Gold Coast Councillor Peter Young, who appeared on the Four Corners program, for defamation.

Cr Tate says Cr Young's motivation for badmouthing him is residual from the 2012 mayoral race in which Cr Young polled 11.9 per cent of the vote. Cr Tate campaigning as an independent won with 37.05 per cent. Elvis Impersonator Dean Vegas polled 9.22 per cent. His supporters commiserated with him in the Heartbreak Hotel, down by the riverside. 'I ain't gonna study war no more,' Mr Vegas said and, indeed, he did not run in 2016.

Mr Tate lost the mayoralty race in 2008 when he ran for the Liberal Party. After winning as an independent in 2012, he was returned as Mayor in 2016 with 63.86 per cent. In his evidence to the CCC, Cr Tate explained how voters do not like party politics at council elections.

Cultural commentator Cr Tate gave his opinion on Facebook of reformed and touring rock group Midnight Oil with frontman, Peter Garrett. The Oils singer, famed for his eccentric versions of pogo dancing, was, in another lifetime, Environment Minister in a Kevin Rudd Labor Government.

Cr Tate posted of Garrett, 'an ozzy version of (U2's) Bono . . . I think he found out it's easier to whinge from the sidelines then to actually be the decision maker as a Minister.'

That's one interpretation of it. Another is Garrett's gig with Labor was always going to end in tears after it began with Garrett having to repudiate his opposition to the American spy base Pine Gap, south-west of Alice Springs in the centre of Australia. It's a long way to the top of a major political party unless you rock and roll to the prevalent winds. (RIP, ACDC's Malcolm Young, thanks for the rhythmic riffs.)

Critics say Pine Gap is a missile and armed drone guidance facility which helped kill tens of thousands of civilians in Iraq. Others say Pine Gap makes Australia a nuclear target. Pundits say a week is a long time in politics. That makes what Peter Garret said two decades before he joined the Labor Party equivalent to a reversion to the Enlightenment.

'It is our intention to give 12-months notice of termination of the above (Pine Gap) agreement on the 19th day of October 1986,' Garrett told a media gathering in that year. 'I don't believe that Pine Gap should be closed,' Garrett told a media gathering in June, 2004. 'I'm fully prepared to accept the position that Labor has taken.'

Garrett then slapped the back of the Boogeymen standing beside him to explain the Labor position. That Boogeyman was named Terrorism with a drop-cap T. Pine Gap was critical to the War on Terrorism – drop-cap W, drop-cap T.

It is, of course, rational for someone to change their mind once receiving new information or appraising changed circumstances. It was just that in Garrett's case the timing was coincidental. In any case, everyone has the right to be wrong.

Garrett joining the Labor Party was a surprise but the independent Mayor Cr Tate having joined a conservative party long ago was not.

The Mayor defined the relationship between his independence and his political loyalty. His chosen medium was Facebook. 'I don't favour one party over another – as mayor I have to work with all sides of politics however I am a life-long member of the LNP,' he posted. (He is a life member but lifelong is a bit of a stretch. Even sixty years ago, you could not be baptized into the Liberal Party.) 'However I wear a gold tie and applaud and support whomever does right by the Goldie. That makes me a Gold (sic) tie essentially,' Cr Tate concluded.

If the Mayor was facilitating a Council meeting, its chair would be a gold tie. That has to be a cartoonist's dream.

Transcript #15
Abridged by Bernie Dowling

Witness Tom Tate, April 26, 2017
PO, Presiding Officer Alan MacSporran QC
CA, Counsel Assisting, Glen Rice QC
W, Tom Tate

CA Is your name Thomas Richard Tate?
W Yes, it is.
CA Mr Tate, you're the current Mayor of Gold Coast City Council?
W Yes, I am.
CA You were first elected to that position in 2012?
W That's correct.
CA And re-elected in 2016?
W Yes, I am.
CA Mr Tate, are you a member of the Liberal National Party?
W Yes, I am.
CA In fact, you're a life member; is that correct?
W That's correct.
CA I've asked you about the 2012 and 2016 elections, but in fact you first contested the mayoralty for the Gold Coast in 2008; is that correct?

W That's correct.

CA In what circumstances did that come about, can you tell us?

W I was approached at the time by the Liberal Party, so that was before the amalgamation (to form the LNP), and I was asked if I was interested to run as a Liberal mayoral candidate, and I didn't respond for quite some months. I actually took time to go to the Rugby World Cup. And by the time I got back, had another meeting.

CA So were there 14 Liberal Party endorsed candidates running on a ticket?

W That's correct.

CA You weren't successful on that occasion?

W No, I was not.

CA To what extent was the team of 14 successful?

W None.

CA None?

W No. Well, the electorate, people of the Gold Coast, voted that they don't want party politics.

(So what happens if a candidate is forced to declare party membership for a level playing field with councillors who complete an interests register? Is there not a real possibility of an uneven playing field with a party (or union) member disadvantaged?)

CA That was the message you took away?

W Absolutely, and democracy has spoken, and I went, "Well" - it was a surprise to me, of course. So the chapter closed at that time with party politics.

CA Do you promote yourself as an independent Mayor?

W I just promote myself as me. I just speak the way I speak. I tell them what's in my heart and my head and don't cloud it. So if some of my beliefs are consistent with conservative, so be it, but at times it may be consistent with Labor Party, you know, let's say the transport infrastructure matters, so we get on well on that part of it. So I put it to you this way: some people try to label me blue tie, being conservative. My response is that I wear gold tie, for the Gold Coast.

CA Can I ask you about campaign funding and take the 2016 campaign to illustrate. How was your campaign funded, Mr Tate?

W Well, it's fully self-funded by my wife, Ruth, and myself. Out of our own bank account, it's a little bit over $182,000.

CA Do you choose not to fundraise?

W I believe that – yes, I do, and, of course, with – the decision is made jointly with your wife.

   (Why would Cr Tate ask Mr Rice's wife?)

CA Did you get assistance of that kind with volunteers?

W I think there was a lot of – we garnished a lot of volunteers that had never done handing out How to Vote Cards before, because, as I went to various booths, a lot of people came up and said, "You know this is the first time I ever handed out for anyone."

CA How did you get enough volunteers?

W It's a bit of a trade secret, but I'll share it with you. You know, what you do is that – I ran a pretty good high-profile Facebook and I would say the majority of that are people who have been following me on Facebook for the last three or four years, and I put out there that I need help, and they will register and go to –

(Yes, we have seen your work in Facebook, Mr Tate, even the music reviews.)

CA One common feature of a number of candidates was the use of SHAC Communications, and you in fact used SHAC Communications for your campaign, did you not?

W Yes, I did.

CA You know Simone Holzapfel?

W Yes, I do.

CA For how long have you known her, Mr Tate?

W '08.

CA She assisted you with that campaign?

W Yes, she did.

CA And each campaign since?

W Yes, she did.

CA Were you aware that other candidates for the 2016 campaign used the services of her business?

W Not first-hand. I read about it in the local paper that somebody has engaged SHAC Communications, another candidate. I never raised it with Simone. That's her business. And I didn't discuss policy of anyone else. But, you know, if other people decided to use SHAC Communications, well, good luck to them.

CA It wasn't by any arrangement with you?

W Nobody arranged anything with me.

CA One of the requirements on candidates, Mr Tate, is to use for campaign purposes a dedicated bank account.

W Yes.

CA You had a bank account styled as Tom Tate Mayoral Account, did you?

W Yes, I do.

CA Can I suggest to you that you and your wife actually used a Westpac bank account for campaign purposes?

W Yes, we do, and we use – we got NAB as well, I think. Our Visa Card is NAB or something.

CA It shouldn't have happened that way, do you accept?

W I accept that.

CA But would you not have been aware of the requirement to maintain a dedicated campaign bank account? I mean, the fact that you had a mayoral account suggests that you were.

W At that time, not until I read later on the disclosure guidelines, which is post the election, you don't have to disclose X number of weeks after, and that's when – the time that I went, well, we should have operated one account, even though it's your own money.

CA Yes.

W So it is a very unique set of circumstances, but I acknowledge, Mr Rice, that it's a better way of doing it, or the correct way of doing it.

CA Well, it's the lawful way of doing it, isn't it?

W Okay, I agree.

27

THE OPERATION BELCARRA REPORT of October 4, 2017, did not recommend prosecution of a number of councillors who appeared to breach electoral laws in 2016 but the CCC recommended welcome reforms and increased enforcement.

Unfortunately, the deferring of punishment to next time under new laws is like the pub offering free beer tomorrow. When the patrons line up for free booze the next day, all they get is the tasteless paradox that tomorrow always comes and never comes.

Employees, whistle-blowers, and journalists exposing corruption are often punished for their good deeds, yet those exposed endure a lashing with the cat o' nine lettuce leaves. For those of us thirsting for prosecutions next time, when the inevitable infringements happen, we have to hope the laws are well constructed and there is the will to enforce them. As the CCC pointed out, some electoral laws operating in 2016 had the infringement use-by-date of 12 months after the offences were committed. When the new seven-day disclosure laws were first tested at the Ipswich by election, they were found wanting and easily circumvented to prevent donation disclosure until after the election. The CCC has recommended a plug for the loophole. But it is not a good sign the State Government lawyers got it wrong the first time and we need extra changes a few months later.

For reasons beyond the ken of my six-month legal career, political donations are referred to as gifts in legislations. But not in my book. If you are a reader of legal sentiment, please read donation as gift.

CCC operation Belcarra recommendations include:

- All expenditure incurred by candidates, their agents, or third parties, must be declared within seven days or immediately if the expenditure is incurred within the seven business days before polling day.
- All expenditure disclosures are made publicly available by the ECQ as soon as practicable, or immediately if the disclosure is provided within the seven business days before polling day.
- Candidates, groups of candidates, third parties, political parties and associated entities cannot receive donations or loans in respect of an election within the seven business days before polling day for that election and at any time thereafter.
- A donation made by an individual must include details of the individual's occupation and employer (if applicable). Donations by a company must include the names and residential or business addresses of the company's directors and a description of the nature of the company's business.
- Donors must declare any business or other connections with councils and councillors.

- Planning applications must include the names and residential or business addresses of a company's directors and details of any political donations.
- Ban donations from developers and construction companies.
- Conduct an inquiry into expenditure caps, including differential caps for incumbent and new candidates.
- All candidates should complete an interests register. Failure to do so would mean that a person is not properly nominated as a candidate.
- Tighten up the definition of a group of candidates, defined by the behaviours of the group and/or its members.
- All recipients of donations within seven business days of receiving a donation requiring a third party return must notify the donor of their disclosure obligations.
- The Electoral Commission of Queensland (ECQ) revises all written information it gives candidates, third parties or others about their obligations in local government elections to ensure that these obligations are clearly communicated in plain English.
- Attending a Local Government Department information session is a mandatory requirement of nomination.
- Candidates and groups of candidates cannot use a credit card to pay for campaign expenses. Candidates can use a debit cards attached to their dedicated account.

- The ECQ, on its website, provide search and analytical tools to allow the investigation of donations.
- Councillors will decide whether one of their number has a real or perceived conflict of interest and their deliberations will be minuted.
- Severe penalties will apply if a councillor infringes on responsibilities regarding conflict of interest.
- Prosecutions for offences related to dedicated accounts and groups of candidates may be started at any time within four years of when the offence was committed, consistent with the current limitation period for offences about disclosure returns.
- Penalties for offences should be increased and the ECQ given statutory power to enforce these penalties.

FOR THE MOST PART, these recommendations are excellent, but, as a sage once said, the proof of the pudding is in the eating, and the devil haunts the detail. And I offer a piece of advice for those framing the new laws. Once you have worded the law, ask yourself in what ways might an unscrupulous person infringe the spirit but not the letter of the law. Believe it or not, naughty nasty unscrupulous people are out there, living in, and perhaps digging up, a street near you.

28

MY WIFE DISLIKES the term 'mum and dad investors' implying as it does financial naivety. Doubtless she would also disdain the notion that councillors are 'mum and dad politicians' equally condescending. I am not forgiving of 'mum and dad' candidates or councillors who cannot follow the basic rules of governance. The rules of approving a multi-million dollar development are sure to be more complex. If self-styled independents are not up to it, maybe it is time to welcome groups back into the administrative tent.

The LGAQ CEO Greg Hallam is a fervent supporter of independents, but he lists the problems they bring to local government. We could draw up their strengths and weaknesses on a sheet of butcher's paper, the mum-and-dad alternative to the electronic whiteboard. First we would need to revisit Mr Hallam's thoughts on the matter:

'We are the level of government closest to the people. A lot of folks do not have a background in understanding the separation of powers, the operations of government, the executive, the judiciary or even the most rudimentary ideas about how governments work. They are motivated because they want to serve their community. So in that sense, we're most reflective of society, I guess, and the corollary of that is that we're probably in some ways least prepared.'

Against all the things a councillor is deficient in we have councillors most reflective of society. But they are not really. Progressives in the community have never been proportionally represented on Moreton Bay Regional Council or Pine Rivers Shire Council before it. Progressives have deferred to conservatives in running community bodies. Perhaps they think office or being in authority is tainted and they prefer to be in unofficial opposition raising community issues as they come along.

When a community bank was set up in Pine Rivers, conservatives dominated the steering committee. Conservatives dominate the service clubs and many other community groups. These groups can be power bases for candidates seeking public office.

Public office is partly vested and partly voted on. The 2016 Moreton Bay Council election shows the process of investiture. Three councillors from the Pine Rivers district retired before the election. They were in the Pine Rivers Shire Council before Moreton Bay and none had tasted electoral defeat since they were first elected in the 1990s. All were conservatives. For some reason the three decided to each champion a candidate for their division. One division already had a conservative candidate nominated but the divisional retiree decided he preferred an alternative conservative who subsequently nominated.

The three candidates championed by the retirees all won. I really scratched my head over that result. I would have thought the community would have welcomed the opportunity for new blood and new thinking. But no, the law of political inertia – a councillor in office will tend to remain in office – was proven again.

It is not a level playing field. If you are a councillor, you can make sure a community group gets a grant and, hey presto, you have troops to hand out your how to vote cards every four years. You have the same heavily-trafficked prime locations for your election signs. You have access to clubs, societies, and retirement villages to spruik your wares. You have other sitting councillors to co-promote with. You will have had the opportunity to be in the local newspaper on a number of occasions over the weeks, months and years before Election Day. You send out your monthly divisional newsletter. If you are smart, you attend many events on a weekend, only staying a few minutes at a time, but saying hello to people you know and introducing yourself to those you do not. Who needs to read those difficult boring electoral acts to get yourself elected and re-elected?

I concede the virtue of having civic-minded councillors as expressed by Mr Hallam. 'They are motivated because they want to serve their community and/or they have some particular issue that they want to address.'

But isn't this an argument for part-time councillors serving a maximum of two or three terms? Have partial elections, like they do in the Senate, and you have a mix of new and old blood on council. Former Ipswich Mayor Paul Pisasale said two of 800 planning decisions went to Council. Do we need full-time councillors for that workload? Work, like nature, abhors a vacuum and it will fill any space allocated to it. Perhaps it is a good system where public servants make planning decisions, assisted by public information and opinion brought to the decision makers by councillors. Australia's public services used to have an excellent reputation for honesty and fairness before it slowly tarnished since 1980 from contact with politicians bearing 'gifts' of economic rationalism. Political interference, possibly by councillors, has been a bigger problem than partiality of public servants. If we want to maintain independent representatives, perhaps we should join the other states which have part-time councillors.

If, on the other hand, we feel we need full-time checks and balances on the administrative arm of Council, parties are a more efficient means of grappling with the complexities of legislation and governance. A couple of party lawyers can read the electoral act or the town plans and translate them into plain English for candidates and councillors. Public funding of local government elections could lead to the re-emergence of parties. Parties would likely have slim pickings for a couple of elections but I am confident they would achieve success after that.

With part-time councillors you can have a lot more of them for the same price as a handful of full-timers representing large areas containing possibly competing communities of interest. Limited term, part-time councillors, in some instances, could be drawn from talented retirees, hopefully not the cranky ones. So this is my gratuitous submission to the CCC: if you want independents in council, make the job part-time and of limited duration. If you want full-time councillors, encourage parties or groups.

It is, after all, residents' groups and community groups keeping vigilance on councils. Even the individual watcher usually finds it effective to seek out the like-minded. This is, in essence, the origins of government and civic administration. It should not surprise to see groups come together to act as a review panel of that government and administration. Authorities can demean them as an unelected rag-tag bunch as much as they like. Citizens groups are not going away any time soon. They are on the rise.

During my journalistic career, I always considered it part of my job to present the reasoned arguments of residents' groups to the general public for weighing up. I had faith in the wisdom of the readership.

Search for other works by Bernie Dowling
Iraqi Icicle, a novel in hardback, paperback, and eBook
7 Shouts, the My *Shout* columns, eBook
Naughty Nineties, Steele Hill tales, eBook
O Lorde, In Her Own Words, eBook

Short story collections, as contributor and co-editor
Redemption, hardback, paperback, and eBook
Can you believe it . . . , eBook
Serendipity, eBook
Alpha and Omega, eBook
Sweet and Sour, eBook
Inspired By . . . , eBook

If you would like a free copy of one of our short stories or would like to comment on any of these books,
Please email: bentbananabooks@gmail.com
Reviews of these works at Amazon, Goodreads or blogs are much appreciated.

Printed by Libri Plureos GmbH in Hamburg, Germany